Pancakes and Waffles

Discover Delicious Pancake Recipes and Waffle Recipes for Amazing Breakfasts in an asy Breakfast Cookbook

By
BookSumo Press
All rights reserved

Published by
http://www.booksumo.com

ENJOY THE RECIPES?

KEEP ON COOKING
WITH 6 MORE FREE COOKBOOKS!

Visit our website and simply enter your email address to join the club and receive your 6 cookbooks.

http://booksumo.com/magnet

https://www.instagram.com/booksumopress/

https://www.facebook.com/booksumo/

LEGAL NOTES

All Rights Reserved. No Part Of This Book May Be Reproduced Or Transmitted In Any Form Or By Any Means. Photocopying, Posting Online, And / Or Digital Copying Is Strictly Prohibited Unless Written Permission Is Granted By The Book's Publishing Company. Limited Use Of The Book's Text Is Permitted For Use In Reviews Written For The Public.

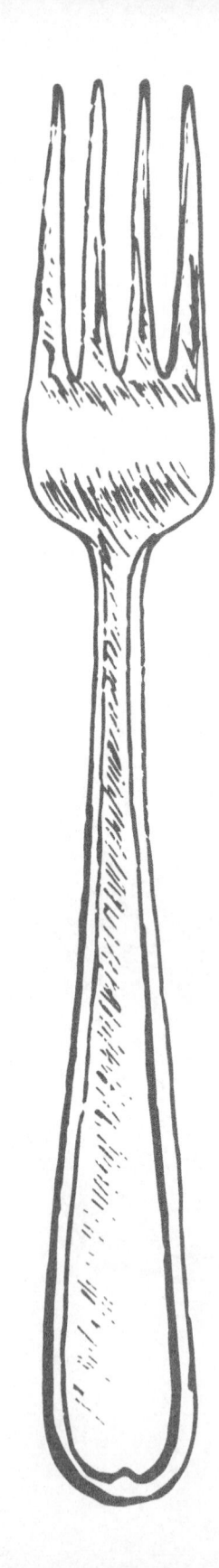

Table of Contents

Manitoba Molasses Waffles 9

How to Make Waffle Batter 10

Belgian Wheat Waffles 11

Brown Rice Potato Waffles 12

Spice Mid-Autumn Waffles 13

West Virginia French Toast Waffles 14

Kentucky Blueberry Waffles 15

Spiced Cardamom Waffl 16

Sourdough Waffles 17

Pecan Honey Oat Waffles 18

Moonlight Waffles 19

Buttermilk Gingerbread Waffles 20

Kindergarten Lunch Box Waffles 21

Carol's Cornmeal Waffles 22

State Fair Waffles 23

3-Grains Oatmeal Waffles 24

Mexican Hash Brown Waffles 25

Houston Waffles 26

Cinnamon Pinwheel Waffles 27

Belgian Waffles 101 28

Madison Oat Waffles 29

Enhanced Toasted Waffles 30

Ice Cream Waffle Sandwiches 31

Country Cottage Waffles 32

Banana Waffles with Extras 33

Sweetened Flax Waffles 35

Victorian Waffles 36

Yam Waffles 37

Twin City Waffles 38

Light Oat Waffles 39

Vegan Almond Waffles 40

Crispy Waffles 101 41

How to Make a Liege Waffle 42

July's Zesty Waffles 43

Apple, Walnuts, and Pumpkin Waffles 44

Florida Duplex Waffles with Vanilla Syrup 45

Waffles Stockholm 46

Gingery Pumpkin Waffles 47

Willie Mae's Buttermilk Waffles 48

Rochester Lemon Waffles 49

Spelman Seltzer Waffles 50

London Butterscotch Waffles 51

Waffles Augusta Autumn 52

Corn on Oats Waffles 53

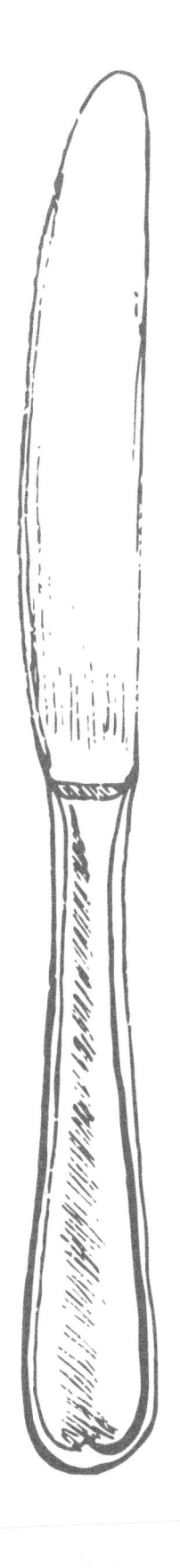

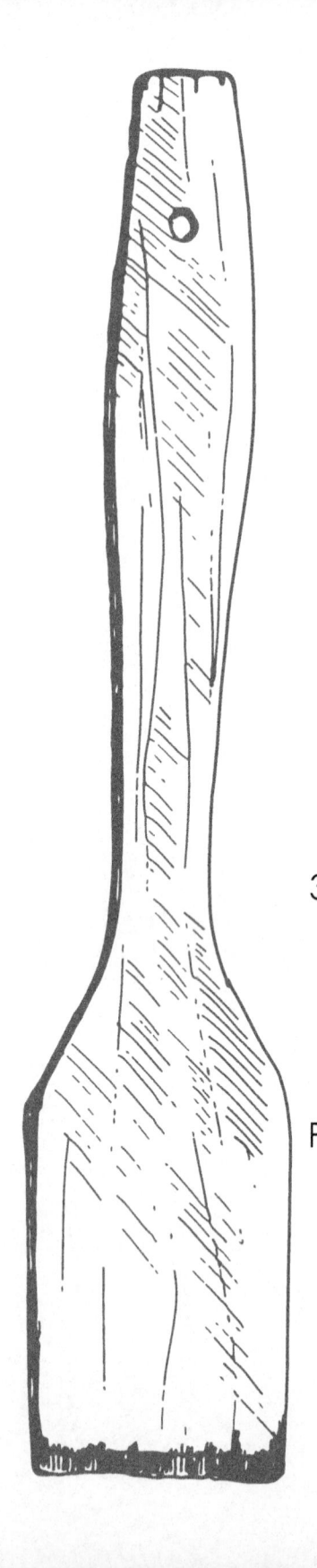

Coffee Bisquick Waffles 54

Poppy Seed Waffles 55

Citrus Waffles 57

Choco Chip Waffles 58

Alternative Pancakes 59

Pancakes for Autumn 60

Dutch Pancakes 61

Light Pancakes 62

Sourdough Pancakes 63

Potato Pancakes 64

Authentic Austrian Pancakes 65

Traditional Swedish Pancakes 66

March Brunch Pancakes 67

3-Ingredient Fruit Banana Pancakes 68

Turkish Pancakes 69

Healthy Breakfast Pancakes 70

Apple Cinnamon Pancakes 71

Peanut Butter Chocolate Pancakes 72

Chicken Pancakes 73

True Tuscan Pancakes 74

Buckwheat Buttermilk Pancakes 75

Almond Amaranth Pancakes 76

Pancakes in Scotland 77

Buttermilk Oat Pancakes 78

Wednesday's Breakfast Pancakes 79

December's German Pancakes 80

How to Make a Pancake 81

Potato Buttermilk Pancakes 82

Friday's Flax Blueberry Pancakes 83

Gourmet Pancake Crepes 84

Zucchini Cheddar Pancakes 85

Russian Breakfast Pancakes 86

Louisiana Inspired Pancakes 87

October's Pancakes 88

Rustic Country Squash Pancakes 89

October's Pancakes 90

Loveable Fruity Pancakes 91

Garden Zucchini Pancakes 92

Swedish Breakfast 93

I ♥ Pancakes 94

Tropical Coconut Pancakes 95

Traditional Chinese Pancakes 96

Parsnip Pancakes 97

South Indian Pancakes 98

Spinach Pancakes 99

Carrot Pancakes 100

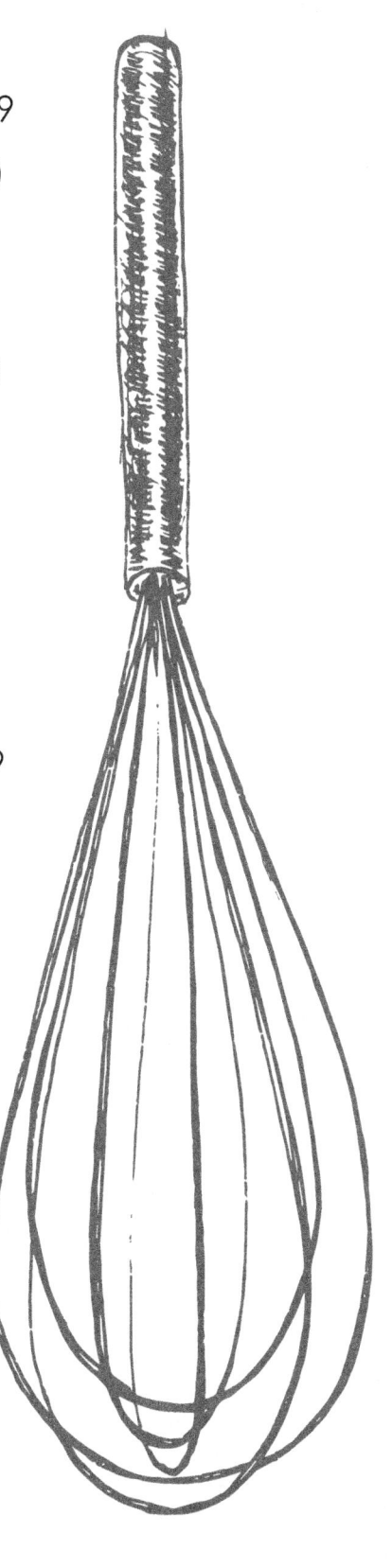

Veggie Combo Pancakes 101

Spicy Buffalo Chicken Pancakes 102

Country Cottage Pancakes 103

South African Pancakes 104

Cocoa Chocolate Pancakes 105

Northern California Pancakes 106

Sweet Pea Pancakes 107

Simple Summer Pesto 108

Manitoba Molasses Waffles

Prep Time: 4 mins
Total Time: 10 mins

Servings per Recipe: 1
Calories   105.7
Fat   2.4g
Cholesterol   18.6mg
Sodium   351.4mg
Carbohydrates   17.6g
Protein   3.4g

Ingredients

2 C. quick oats
1/2 C. flour
1 tsp salt
1 1/2 C. water
1 tbsp baking powder

1 beaten egg
1 tbsp molasses
2 tbsp corn oil

Directions

1. Set your waffle iron and lightly, grease it.
2. In a bowl, add all ingredients and mix until well combined.
3. Add desired amount of the mixture in waffle iron and cook as suggested by the manufacturer.
4. Repeat with the remaining mixture.
5. Enjoy warm.

HOW TO
Waffle Batter

Prep Time: 10 mins
Total Time: 20 mins

Servings per Recipe: 6
Calories 345.2
Fat 16.5g
Cholesterol 71.4mg
Sodium 433.1mg
Carbohydrates 39.9g
Protein 8.6g

Ingredients

2 eggs
1 2/3 C. milk
1/3 C. vegetable oil
2 C. all-purpose flour
1 tbsp baking powder

2 tbsp sugar
1/2 tsp salt
1 tsp vanilla
1 tsp maple extract

Directions

1. Set your waffle iron and lightly, grease it.
2. In a bowl, mix together the flour, sugar, baking powder and salt.
3. In another bowl, add remaining ingredients and beat until well combined.
4. Add flour mixture and mix until just combined.
5. Add desired amount of the mixture in waffle iron and cook as suggested by the manufacturer.
6. Repeat with the remaining mixture.
7. Enjoy warm.

Belgian Wheat Waffles

Prep Time: 5 mins
Total Time: 45 mins

Servings per Recipe: 16
Calories   137.3
Fat   6.9g
Cholesterol   39.1mg
Sodium   205.7mg
Carbohydrates   15.6g
Protein   4.1g

Ingredients

2 C. whole wheat flour
1/4 C. sugar
3 tsp baking powder
3/4 tsp salt
2 C. milk

3 eggs
1/3 C. vegetable oil
1 tsp vanilla extract

Directions

1. Set your waffle iron and lightly, grease it.
2. In a bowl, add the flour, baking powder, sugar and salt and mix well.
3. Add the eggs, oil, and milk and stir until blended.
4. Add about 1/3 C. of the mixture into the waffle iron and cook as suggested by the manufacturer.
5. Repeat with the remaining mixture.
6. Enjoy warm.

BROWN RICE
Potato Waffles

Prep Time: 8 mins
Total Time: 23 mins

Servings per Recipe: 1
Calories	352.5
Fat	14.5g
Cholesterol	77.3mg
Sodium	727.3mg
Carbohydrates	46.8g
Protein	8.9g

Ingredients

- 1 C. brown rice flour
- 1/2 C. potato starch
- 1/4 C. tapioca flour
- 2 tsp baking powder
- 1 tsp salt
- 1/4 C. oil
- 2 eggs
- 1 1/2 C. buttermilk
- 1 tsp sugar

Directions

1. In a bowl, add all the ingredients and mix until well combined.
2. Add desired amount of the mixture in waffle iron and cook as suggested by the manufacturer.
3. Repeat with the remaining mixture.
4. Enjoy warm.

Spice Mid-Autumn Waffles

🥣 Prep Time: 10 mins
🕐 Total Time: 15 mins

Servings per Recipe: 1
Calories   227.1
Fat   9.2g
Cholesterol   68.8mg
Sodium   403.8mg
Carbohydrates   30.5g
Protein   6.1g

Ingredients

1 1/2 C. all-purpose flour
3 tsp baking powder
1/2 tsp baking soda
1 tsp cinnamon
1 tsp nutmeg
1 tsp ground ginger
1 pinch salt

2 eggs
1/4 C. packed brown sugar
1 C. canned pumpkin puree
1 2/3 C. milk
4 tbsp butter, melted and cooled

Directions

1. In a bowl, add the flour, baking soda, baking powder, spices and salt and mix well.
2. In another bowl, add milk, eggs, butter, sugar and pumpkin and beat until well combined.
3. Add the flour mixture and mix until just combined.
4. Add desired amount of the mixture in waffle iron and cook as suggested by the manufacturer.
5. Repeat with the remaining mixture.
6. Enjoy warm.

WEST VIRGINIA
French Toast Waffles

Prep Time: 5 mins
Total Time: 9 mins

Servings per Recipe: 2
Calories 329.3
Fat 19.2g
Cholesterol 246.3mg
Sodium 507.2mg
Carbohydrates 27.1g
Protein 11.2g

Ingredients

4 -6 slices thick-sliced bread, trimmed
2 eggs, beaten
1/4 C. milk
2 tbsp butter, melted
1/4 tsp vanilla
1/4 tsp cinnamon

Directions

1. Set your waffle iron and lightly, grease it.
2. In a shallow dish, add the butter, milk, eggs, vanilla and cinnamon and beat until well combined.
3. Coat each bread slices with egg mixture evenly.
4. Arrange the bread slices in waffle iron and cook until golden brown.
5. Enjoy warm with a topping of your favorite condiments.

Kentucky Blueberry Waffles

Prep Time: 10 mins
Total Time: 20 mins

Servings per Recipe: 1
Calories   305.7
Fat   11.9g
Cholesterol   90.8mg
Sodium   497.5mg
Carbohydrates   40.9g
Protein   8.6g

Ingredients

- 1 C. blueberries
- 3 tsp baking powder
- 2 eggs, separated
- 1 tbsp sugar
- 2 C. sifted flour
- 1 1/2 C. milk
- 1/2 tsp salt
- 1/4 C. melted butter

Directions

1. Set your waffle iron and lightly, grease it.
2. In a glass bowl, add the egg whites and beat until stiff peak form.
3. In a bowl, add the flour, baking powder and salt and mix well.
4. Now, sift the flour mixture in a second bowl.
5. In a third bowl, add the butter, egg yolks and milk and beat until well combined.
6. Slowly, add the butter mixture into the flour mixture, beating continuously until well combined.
7. Add the blueberries and gently, stir to combine.
8. Gently, fold the whipped egg whites into the flour mixture.
9. Add desired amount of the mixture in waffle iron and cook as suggested by the manufacturer.
10. Repeat with the remaining mixture.
11. Enjoy warm.

SPICED Cardamom Waffles

Prep Time: 5 mins
Total Time: 30 mins

Servings per Recipe: 4
Calories	452.3
Fat	24.8g
Cholesterol	151.9mg
Sodium	627.7mg
Carbohydrates	45.7g
Protein	11.2g

Ingredients

1 1/2 C. flour
1 1/2 tsp baking powder
3/4 tsp baking soda
1/4 tsp salt, rounded
1 tsp ground cardamom
1 C. whole milk
1 C. sour cream

1 tsp pure vanilla extract
1 tbsp mild honey
2 large eggs
3 tbsp unsalted butter, melted
powdered sugar

Directions

1. Set your waffle iron and lightly, grease it.
2. In a bowl, add the flour, baking soda, baking powder, cardamom and salt and mix well.
3. In a separate bowl, add the remaining ingredients and beat until well combined.
4. Add the flour mixture and mix until just blended.
5. Add desired amount of the mixture in waffle iron and cook as suggested by the manufacturer.
6. Repeat with the remaining mixture.
7. Enjoy with a dusting of the powdered sugar.

Sourdough Waffles

Prep Time: 5 mins
Total Time: 10 mins

Servings per Recipe: 3
Calories   247.8
Fat   11.3g
Cholesterol   62.0mg
Sodium   624.1mg
Carbohydrates   30.4g
Protein   6.8g

Ingredients

- 1/2 C. sourdough starter
- 1/2 C. whole wheat flour
- 1/2 C. any whole grain flour
- 1 C. water
- 1 egg
- 2 tbsp oil
- 1/2 tsp salt
- 1/2 tsp baking soda

Directions

1. In a bowl, add the flours, starter and water and mix until well combined.
2. With a plastic sheet, cover the bowl and keep aside for 12 hours.
3. Set your waffle iron and lightly, grease it.
4. In the bowl of the flour mixture, add the oil, salt and egg and mix until well combined.
5. Add the baking soda just before the cooking.
6. Add about 1/4 C. of the mixture in waffle iron and cook for about 5 minutes.
7. Repeat with the remaining mixture.
8. Enjoy warm.

PECAN
Honey Oat Waffles

Prep Time: 10 mins
Total Time: 15 mins

Servings per Recipe: 1
Calories   247.4
Fat   13.8g
Cholesterol   51.1mg
Sodium   217.3mg
Carbohydrates   25.7g
Protein   7.5g

Ingredients

1 1/2 C. whole wheat flour
2 tsp baking powder
1/2 tsp salt
2 C. milk
2 eggs
1/4 C. melted butter
2 tbsp honey

1 C. uncooked oats
1 C. pecans, chopped

Directions

1. Set your waffle iron and lightly, grease it.
2. In a bowl, add the flour, baking powder and salt and mix well.
3. Add the butter, milk, honey and eggs and with an electric mixer, beat on medium speed until well combined.
4. Gently, fold in the oats and pecans.
5. Add desired amount of the mixture in waffle iron and cook for about 5 minutes.
6. Repeat with the remaining mixture.
7. Enjoy warm.

Moonlight Waffles

Prep Time: 9 hrs
Total Time: 9 hrs 5 mins

Servings per Recipe: 4
Calories   558.7
Fat   30.5g
Cholesterol   171.1mg
Sodium   590.2mg
Carbohydrates   56.9g
Protein   14.0g

Ingredients

- 1/2 tsp instant yeast
- 2 C. all-purpose flour
- 1 tbsp sugar
- 1/2 tsp salt
- 2 C. milk
- 8 tbsp melted butter
- 1/2 tsp vanilla
- lite olive oil
- 2 eggs, separated

Directions

1. In a bowl, add the flour, yeast, sugar and salt and mix well.
2. Add the butter, milk and vanilla and mix until well combined.
3. With a plastic wrap, cover the bowl and keep aside for the whole night.
4. In the bowl of the flour mixture, add the yolks and mix well.
5. In another bowl, add the egg whites and beat until soft peaks form.
6. Gently fold the whipped whites into the flour mixture.
7. Set your waffle iron and lightly, grease it.
8. Add desired amount of the mixture in waffle iron and cook for about 4-5 minutes.
9. Repeat with the remaining mixture.
10. Enjoy warm.

BUTTERMILK Gingerbread Waffles

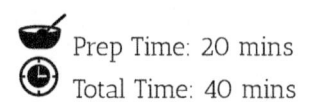

Prep Time: 20 mins
Total Time: 40 mins

Servings per Recipe: 8
Calories   314.0
Fat   7.7g
Cholesterol   63.6mg
Sodium   454.1mg
Carbohydrates   55.4g
Protein   6.4g

Ingredients

4 tbsp butter, melted
2 C. flour
1 tbsp baking powder
3/4 tsp baking soda
1/4 tsp salt
1 tbsp ground ginger
3/4 tsp cinnamon
1/4 tsp ground cloves
1/4 tsp ground nutmeg
3/4 C. brown sugar
1 1/2 C. buttermilk
1/4 C. molasses
2 eggs, beaten

Directions

1. Set your waffle iron and lightly, grease it.
2. In a bowl, add the flour, baking soda, baking powder, brown sugar, spices and salt and mix well.
3. Now, sift the flour mixture into another bowl.
4. In a third bowl, add the molasses, buttermilk and egg and beat until well combined.
5. Add the melted butter and mix well.
6. Add the flour mixture and mix until just combined.
7. Add desired amount of the mixture in waffle iron and cook as suggested by the manufacturer.
8. Repeat with the remaining mixture.
9. Enjoy warm.

Kindergarten
Lunch Box Waffles

Prep Time: 5 mins
Total Time: 6 mins

Servings per Recipe: 6
Calories 692.7
Fat 34.9g
Cholesterol 205.3mg
Sodium 707.0mg
Carbohydrates 86.1g
Protein 10.1g

Ingredients

1 C. butter
4 beaten eggs
1 1/2 C. sugar
1/2 C. cocoa
2 C. flour

1 tsp vanilla
1 tsp salt
1/2 C. water

Directions

1. Set your waffle iron to medium setting and lightly, grease it.
2. In a bowl, add all the ingredients and mix until well combined.
3. Add desired amount of the mixture in waffle iron and cook for about 1 minute.
4. Repeat with the remaining mixture.
5. Enjoy warm.

CAROL'S
Cornmeal Waffles

Prep Time: 5 mins
Total Time: 25 mins

Servings per Recipe: 1
Calories 304.9
Fat 16.9g
Cholesterol 59.2mg
Sodium 368.7mg
Carbohydrates 31.6g
Protein 6.6g

Ingredients

1 egg
3/4 C. milk
1/4 C. vegetable oil
1 C. all-purpose flour
2 tbsp cornmeal

2 tsp baking powder
2 tsp sugar
1/4 tsp salt

Directions

1. Set your waffle iron and lightly, grease it.
2. In a food processor, add all the ingredients and pulse on medium-high speed until just combined.
3. Add 1/2 C. of the e mixture in waffle iron and cook for about 4-5 minutes.
4. Repeat with the remaining mixture.
5. Enjoy warm.

State Fair Waffles

Prep Time: 10 mins
Total Time: 17 mins

Servings per Recipe: 12
Calories   220.6
Fat   10.9g
Cholesterol   47.2mg
Sodium   218.1mg
Carbohydrates   27.6g
Protein   4.9g

Ingredients

- 2 C. all-purpose flour
- 1 C. semi-sweet chocolate chips
- 2 tsp granulated sugar
- 1 tbsp baking powder
- 1/2 tsp salt
- 1/2 tsp cinnamon
- 1 2/3 C. low-fat milk
- 1/3 C. unsalted butter, melted
- 2 extra large eggs, beaten

Directions

1. Set your waffle iron and lightly, grease it.
2. In a bowl, add the flour, sugar, chocolate chips, baking powder, cinnamon and salt and mix well.
3. Add the butter and milk and mix until well combined.
4. Add the eggs and mix until just combined.
5. Add desired amount of the mixture in waffle iron and cook as suggested by the manufacturer.
6. Repeat with the remaining mixture.
7. Enjoy warm.

3-GRAINS
Oatmeal Waffles

Prep Time: 10 mins
Total Time: 20 mins

Servings per Recipe: 15
Calories 207.8
Fat 9.5g
Cholesterol 56.4mg
Sodium 459.6mg
Carbohydrates 24.6g
Protein 6.5g

Ingredients

1 C. whole wheat flour
1 C. cornmeal
1 C. all-purpose flour
1 C. rolled oats
4 tsp baking powder
1 1/2 tsp salt
1 tsp baking soda

3 C. milk
4 eggs
6 tbsp canola oil

Directions

1. In a bowl, add the flours, cornmeal, oats, baking powder, baking soda and salt and mix well.
2. Add the remaining ingredients and mix until well combined.
3. Keep aside for about 5 minutes.
4. Add desired amount of the mixture in waffle iron and cook as suggested by the manufacturer.
5. Repeat with the remaining mixture.
6. Enjoy warm.

Mexican Hash Brown Waffles

Prep Time: 10 mins
Total Time: 30 mins

Servings per Recipe: 4
Calories 407.1
Fat 29.4g
Cholesterol 441.3mg
Sodium 1277.8mg
Carbohydrates 7.9g
Protein 27.7g

Ingredients

2 C. Simply Potatoes® Shredded Hash Browns
1 C. thick & chunky salsa, divided
8 large eggs, divided
2 C. Mexican blend cheese
8 tbsp cilantro, chopped

Directions

1. Set your waffle iron and lightly, grease it.
2. In a bowl, add the 2 eggs, potatoes and 1/3 C. of the salsa and stir until combined nicely.
3. Add the mixture in waffle iron and cook for about 15-20 minutes.
4. Meanwhile, in a bowl, crack the remaining eggs and beat well.
5. Add 1/3 C. of the salsa and stir until combined nicely.
6. For the scrambled eggs, place a nonstick wok over medium heat until heated through.
7. Add the egg mixture and until desired doneness, stirring continuously.
8. Add 1 C. of the cheese and cook, until cheese is melted, stirring continuously.
9. Remove from the heat and top with the remaining cheese evenly.
10. Cut each waffle into four equal sized pieces.
11. Divide waffle pieces onto serving plates and top each with the scrambled eggs, followed by the remaining salsa.
12. Enjoy.

HOUSTON
Waffles

Prep Time: 20 mins
Total Time: 1 hr 20 mins

Servings per Recipe: 1
Calories	213.4
Fat	7.3g
Cholesterol	77.8mg
Sodium	175.5mg
Carbohydrates	30.1g
Protein	6.6g

Ingredients

2 1/2 tsp yeast
2 C. lukewarm milk
4 eggs, separated
1 tsp vanilla
2 1/2 C. flour
1/2 tsp salt
1 tbsp sugar

1/4 C. melted butter
2 C. strawberries, hulled and sliced
1/2 C. powdered sugar

Directions

1. In a bowl, add the warm milk and yeast and mix until well combined.
2. In a second bowl, add the flour, sugar and salt and mix well.
3. In a third bowl, add the egg yolks and beat well.
4. Add the egg yolks and vanilla in the bowl of the yeast mixture and mix well.
5. Add the flour mixture and mix until just combined.
6. Add the melted butter and mix until well combined.
7. In a glass bowl, add the egg whites and beat until stiff peaks form.
8. Gently, fold the whipped egg whites into the flour mixture.
9. Keep aside in the warm area for about 45 minutes.
10. Set your waffle iron and lightly, grease it.
11. Add desired amount of the mixture in waffle iron and cook as suggested by the manufacturer.
12. Repeat with the remaining mixture.
13. Divide the waffles onto serving plates and top each with the strawberries.
14. Enjoy with a dusting of powdered sugar.

Cinnamon Pinwheel Waffles

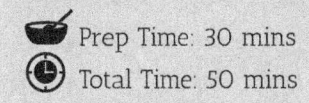

Prep Time: 30 mins
Total Time: 50 mins

Servings per Recipe: 1
Calories	345.5
Fat	19.0g
Cholesterol	68.3mg
Sodium	306.8mg
Carbohydrates	39.8g
Protein	4.7g

Ingredients

Waffles
1 3/4 C. all-purpose flour
2 tbsp granulated sugar
1 tsp baking powder
1/2 tsp baking soda
1/4 tsp salt
2 large eggs
2 C. buttermilk
1/4 C. vegetable oil
1 tsp vanilla extract

Cinnamon Garnish
1/2 C. butter, melted
3/4 C. brown sugar, packed
1 tbsp ground cinnamon

Cheese Garnish
4 tbsp butter
2 oz. cream cheese
3/4 C. powdered sugar
1/2 tsp vanilla extract

Directions

1. For the waffles: in a bowl, add the flour, sugar, baking soda, baking powder and salt.
2. With a spoon, create a well in the middle of the flour mixture.
3. In another bowl, add the oil, buttermilk, eggs and vanilla and beat until well combined.
4. Add the egg mixture in the well of the flour mixture and mix until just combined.
5. Add desired amount of the mixture in waffle iron and cook as suggested by the manufacturer. Repeat with the remaining mixture.
6. Meanwhile, for the cinnamon topping: in a bowl, add the brown sugar, cinnamon and butter and mix until combined.
7. For the cream cheese topping: in a microwave-safe bowl, add the cream cheese and butter and microwave for about 40-60 seconds.
8. Remove from the microwave and stir until smooth.
9. Add the powdered sugar and vanilla extract and beat until well combined.
10. Divide the waffles onto serving plates and top each with the cinnamon topping, followed by the cream cheese topping. Enjoy.

BELGIAN
Waffles 101

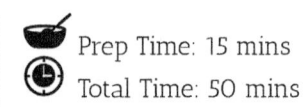

Prep Time: 15 mins
Total Time: 50 mins

Servings per Recipe: 4
Calories   635.9
Fat   34.7g
Cholesterol   110.0mg
Sodium   750.5mg
Carbohydrates   67.2g
Protein   13.6g

Ingredients

2 C. flour
4 tsp baking powder
1/2 tsp salt
1/4 C. sugar
2 eggs

1/2 C. vegetable oil
2 C. milk
1 tsp vanilla

Directions

1. Set your waffle iron to medium-high heat and lightly, grease it.
2. In a bowl, add the flour, sugar, baking powder and salt and mix well.
3. Now, sift the flour mixture into another bowl.
4. In another bowl, add the oil, milk, egg yolks and vanilla and beat until well combined.
5. Add the flour mixture and mix until well combined.
6. In a glass bowl, add the egg whites and beat until stiff peaks form.
7. Gently, fold the whipped egg whites into the flour mixture.
8. Add desired amount of the mixture in waffle iron and cook for about 6-10 minutes.
9. Repeat with the remaining mixture.
10. Enjoy warm.

Madison Oat Waffles

Prep Time: 10 mins
Total Time: 50 mins

Servings per Recipe: 6
Calories   200.8
Fat   8.8g
Cholesterol   28.9mg
Sodium   371.4mg
Carbohydrates   26.8g
Protein   8.4g

Ingredients

3/4 C. oat bran
1/2 C. whole wheat flour
1/2 C. all-purpose flour
2 tsp baking powder
1/2 tsp salt
1 1/2 C. skim milk
3 tbsp vegetable oil

1 egg yolk, beaten
2 egg whites

Directions

1. In a bowl, add the flours, oat bran, baking powder and salt and mix well.
2. In another bowl, add the egg yolk, oil and milk and beat until well combined.
3. Add the flour mixture and mix until just combined.
4. In a glass bowl, add the egg whites and with an electric mixer, beat on high speed until stiff peaks form.
5. Gently, fold the whipped egg whites into the flour mixture.
6. Add desired amount of the mixture in waffle iron and cook as suggested by the manufacturer.
7. Repeat with the remaining mixture.
8. Enjoy warm.

ENHANCED
Toasted Waffles

🥣 Prep Time: 1 min
🕐 Total Time: 5 mins

Servings per Recipe: 4
Calories 576.0
Fat 28.4g
Cholesterol 126.9mg
Sodium 840.8mg
Carbohydrates 68.0g
Protein 13.5g

Ingredients

8 frozen waffles, toasted
3 oz. cream cheese
14 oz. canned peaches
1 tbsp brown sugar

whipped cream

Directions

1. Spread cream cheese over each toasted waffle, followed by the fruit, brown sugar and whipped cream.
2. Enjoy.

Ice Cream Waffle Sandwiches

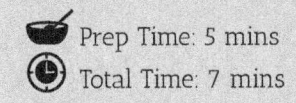

Prep Time: 5 mins
Total Time: 7 mins

Servings per Recipe: 1
Calories   709.7
Fat   35.6g
Cholesterol   161.5mg
Sodium   872.1mg
Carbohydrates   80.5g
Protein   16.4g

Ingredients

2 toasted hot waffles
1 C. ice cream
Toppings
1 - 2 tbsp decorative candies
1 - 2 tbsp crushed nuts
1 - 2 tbsp toasted coconut
1 - 2 tbsp granola cereal
1 - 2 tbsp praline
peanut butter spread on before ice cream

Directions

1. Place a thin layer of the peanut butter over each waffle evenly.
2. Put the ice cream onto inner part of each waffle.
3. Place your favorite topping beside the ice cream.
4. Enjoy.

COUNTRY
Cottage Waffles

Prep Time: 10 mins
Total Time: 20 mins

Servings per Recipe: 1
Calories   312.1
Fat   12.6g
Cholesterol   94.0mg
Sodium   540.3mg
Carbohydrates   38.6g
Protein   11.1g

Ingredients

4 tbsp unsalted butter, melted
1 3/4 C. all-purpose flour
2 tsp baking powder
1/4 tsp baking soda
1/2 tsp salt
1 C. cottage cheese

1 C. milk
2 large eggs
2 1/2 tbsp honey

Directions

1. Set your waffle iron and lightly, grease it.
2. In a bowl, add the flour, baking powder, baking soda and salt and mix well.
3. In another bowl, add the honey, eggs, milk and cottage cheese and beat until just combined.
4. Slowly, add the flour mixture and mix until just combined.
5. Add the butter and stir to combine.
6. Add desired amount of the mixture in waffle iron and cook as suggested by the manufacturer.
7. Repeat with the remaining mixture.
8. Enjoy warm.

Banana Waffles with Extras

🥣 Prep Time: 1 hr
🕐 Total Time: 1 hr

Servings per Recipe: 1
Calories 215.8
Fat 13.0g
Cholesterol 65.2mg
Sodium 130.1mg
Carbohydrates 22.0g
Protein 3.9g

Ingredients

- 1/2 C. pecans, lightly toasted
- 1 1/2 C. flour
- 1/2 C. yellow cornmeal
- 1 tbsp baking powder
- 1/4 tsp salt
- 1 1/4 C. milk
- 3/4 C. unsalted butter, melted
- 3 large eggs, separated
- 2 large ripe bananas, quartered lengthwise and chopped
- 3 tbsp sugar
- 1 tbsp light brown sugar
- 1 small banana, sliced into discs
- maple syrup, warmed

Directions

1. Set your oven to 350 degrees F before doing anything else.
2. In the bottom of a baking sheet, place the pecans in a single layer.
3. Cook in the oven for about 10 minutes.
4. Remove from the oven and keep aside to cool completely.
5. After cooling, chop the pecans roughly. and set aside.
6. In a bowl, add the cornmeal, flour, baking powder and salt and mix well. In another bowl, add the butter, milk and egg yolks and beat until well combined.
7. Gradually, add the butter mixture into the flour mixture until just combined. Gently, fold half of the banana pieces.
8. In a glass bowl, add the egg whites and with an electric mixer, beat on medium speed until fluffy.
9. Now, beat on high speed until firm peaks form.
10. Add both sugars and beat until stiff.
11. Gently, fold the whipped egg whites into the flour mixture.

12. Set your waffle iron and lightly, grease it.
13. Add desired amount of the mixture in waffle iron and cook for about 6 minutes.
14. Repeat with the remaining mixture.
15. Enjoy warm with a topping of the banana slices, pecans and maple syrup.

Sweetened Flax Waffles

Prep Time: 20 mins
Total Time: 20 mins

Servings per Recipe: 1
Calories   125.4
Fat   5.6g
Cholesterol   38.4mg
Sodium   182.0mg
Carbohydrates   14.8g
Protein   4.5g

Ingredients

1 1/2 C. whole wheat flour
1 1/2 C. white flour
1/2 tsp powdered stevia
6 tsp baking powder
4 tbsp flax seeds
1/2 tsp salt
4 eggs
3 C. milk
1/4 C. olive oil

Directions

1. In a bowl, add the flours, flax seed, stevia, baking powder and salt.
2. In another bowl, add the remaining ingredients and beat until well combined.
3. Add the flour mixture and mix until just combined.
4. Add 3/4 C. of the mixture in waffle iron and cook as suggested by the manufacturer.
5. Repeat with the remaining mixture.
6. Enjoy warm.

VICTORIAN
Waffles

Prep Time: 5 mins
Total Time: 45 mins

Servings per Recipe: 1
Calories   165.2
Fat   5.7g
Cholesterol   0.0mg
Sodium   238.0mg
Carbohydrates   24.4g
Protein   4.7g

Ingredients

1 1/2 C. white flour
1 1/2 C. whole wheat flour
1/4 C. flax seed
2 tbsp sugar
1 tbsp baking powder
1 tsp salt

3 C. soy milk
1 large banana, mashed
1/4 C. canola oil
2 tsp vanilla extract

Directions

1. In a bowl, add the flours, flax seed, sugar, baking powder and salt.
2. In another bowl, add the remaining ingredients and beat until well combined.
3. Add the flour mixture and with a hand mixer, beat on a low setting well combined.
4. Heat a waffle iron and spray with oil.
5. Add desired amount of the mixture in waffle iron and cook as suggested by the manufacturer.
6. Repeat with the remaining mixture.
7. Enjoy warm.

Yam Waffles

Prep Time: 10 mins
Total Time: 40 mins

Servings per Recipe: 12
Calories	141.6
Fat	4.6g
Cholesterol	31.6mg
Sodium	157.6mg
Carbohydrates	20.7g
Protein	4.8g

Ingredients

- 1 C. whole wheat flour
- 1 C. all-purpose flour
- 4 tsp baking powder
- 1/2 tsp cinnamon
- 1/4 tsp clove
- 2 eggs, separated
- 1 1/2 C. skim milk
- 1 C. pureed cooked sweet potato
- 3 tbsp oil
- 2 tsp grated orange rind
- 1 tbsp granulated sugar

Directions

1. In a bowl, add the flour, spices and baking powder.
2. In another bowl, add the oil, milk, egg yolks, orange rind and sweet potato and beat until well combined.
3. Add the flour mixture and mix until just combined.
4. In a glass bowl, add the egg whites and with an electric mixer, beat until soft peaks form.
5. Add the sugar and beat until stiff peaks form.
6. Gently, fold the whipped egg whites into the flour mixture.
7. Add desired amount of the mixture in waffle iron and cook for about 5 minutes.
8. Repeat with the remaining mixture.
9. Enjoy warm.

TWIN CITY
Waffles

Prep Time: 15 mins
Total Time: 15 mins

Servings per Recipe: 4
Calories	387.0
Fat	25.0g
Cholesterol	109.0mg
Sodium	488.2mg
Carbohydrates	34.9g
Protein	6.9g

Ingredients

1 C. flour
1 1/2 tsp sugar
1 tsp baking powder
1/4 tsp baking soda
1/4 tsp salt
1 egg, separated

1 C. sour cream
1/4 C. milk
1/4 C. butter, melted
1 banana, mashed

Directions

1. Set your waffle iron and lightly, grease it.
2. In a bowl, add the flour, sugar, baking powder, baking soda and salt and mix well.
3. Now, sift the flour mixture into another bowl.
4. In another bowl, add the butter, milk, sour cream, egg yolk and banana and beat until well combined.
5. Add the flour mixture and mix until blended nicely.
6. In a glass bowl, add the egg whites and beat until stiff peak form.
7. Gently, fold the whipped egg whites into the flour mixture.
8. Add desired amount of the mixture in waffle iron and cook as suggested by the manufacturer.
9. Repeat with the remaining mixture.
10. Enjoy warm.

Light Oat Waffles

🥣 Prep Time: 10 mins
🕐 Total Time: 30 mins

Servings per Recipe: 4
Calories   213.9
Fat   8.9g
Cholesterol   0.0mg
Sodium   473.5mg
Carbohydrates   29.4g
Protein   5.2g

Ingredients

3/4 C. unbleached white flour
1/4 C. whole wheat flour
1/2 tsp salt
2 tsp baking powder
1/8 tsp ground cinnamon
1/8 tsp ground nutmeg
1/4 C. walnuts, chopped toasted

1/4 C. quick-cooking oats
1 1/3 C. vanilla-flavored soy milk
1 tbsp vegetable oil
1 tsp pure maple syrup

Directions

1. Set your oven to 350 degrees F before doing anything else.
2. In the bottom of a baking sheet, place the walnuts in a single layer.
3. Cook in the oven for about 5-10 minutes.
4. Remove from the oven and keep aside to cool completely.
5. In a bowl, add the flours, baking powder, spices and salt and mix well.
6. Now, sift the flour mixture into another bowl.
7. Add the oats and walnuts and stir to combine.
8. In another bowl, add the maple syrup, oil and milk and beat until well combined.
9. With a spoon, create a well in the center of the flour mixture.
10. Add the oil mixture in the well and mix until just blended.
11. Keep aside until bubbles appears on the top of the dough.
12. Set your waffle iron and lightly, grease it.
13. Add 1/3 C. of the mixture in waffle iron and cook as suggested by the manufacturer.
14. Repeat with the remaining mixture.
15. Enjoy warm.

VEGAN
Almond Waffles

Prep Time: 5 mins
Total Time: 10 mins

Servings per Recipe: 6
Calories	299.6
Fat	25.4g
Cholesterol	0.0mg
Sodium	414.4mg
Carbohydrates	15.6g
Protein	5.0g

Ingredients

1 large banana, mashed
1 3/4 C. soy milk
1/2 C. vegetable oil
1 tbsp honey
2 C. gluten-free flour
4 tsp baking powder
1/4 tsp salt
1/2 C. chopped almonds

Directions

1. Set your waffle iron and lightly, grease it.
2. In a bowl, add the oil, soy milk, honey and bananas and with an electric mixer, beat until well combined.
3. Add the baking powder, flour and salt and mix until just combined.
4. Gently, fold in the almonds.
5. Set your waffle iron and lightly, grease it.
6. Add 2/3 C. of the mixture in waffle iron and cook for about 5 minutes.
7. Repeat with the remaining mixture.
8. Enjoy warm.

Crispy Waffles 101

Prep Time: 15 mins
Total Time: 22 mins

Servings per Recipe: 1
Calories	148.5
Fat	7.0g
Cholesterol	24.5mg
Sodium	135.8mg
Carbohydrates	17.4g
Protein	3.6g

Ingredients

- 2 eggs, beaten
- 1 tsp salt
- 1 tbsp sugar
- 1/2 C. vegetable oil
- 2 C. warm milk
- 1 (1/4 oz.) package yeast, dissolved in 1/4 C. water
- 3 1/4 C. flour, sifted

Directions

1. In a bowl, add the oil, eggs, sugar and salt and mix well.
2. In another bowl, add the flour, yeast mixture and warm milk and mix until well combined.
3. With a plastic wrap, cover the bowl and place in the fridge for whole night.
4. Set your waffle iron and lightly, grease it.
5. Add desired amount of the mixture in waffle iron and cook as suggested by the manufacturer.
6. Repeat with the remaining mixture.
7. Enjoy warm.

HOW TO
Make a Liege Waffle

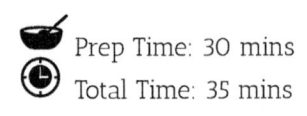

🥣 Prep Time: 30 mins
🕐 Total Time: 35 mins

Servings per Recipe: 4
Calories 904.4
Fat 50.3g
Cholesterol 261.5mg
Sodium 534.2mg
Carbohydrates 103.3g
Protein 12.2g

Ingredients

1 (1/4 oz.) package yeast
1/3 C. lukewarm water
1 1/2 tbsp granulated sugar
1/8 tsp salt
2 C. flour
3 eggs

1 C. softened butter
1 C. pearl sugar

Directions

1. In a bowl, add the sugar, yeast, salt and water and mix until well combined.
2. Keep aside for about 13-15 minutes.
3. In another bowl, add the flour and with a spoon, create a well in the center.
4. Add the yeast mixture in the center with your hands, knead until well combined.
5. Slowly, add the eggs, 1 at a time alongside 2 tbsp of the butter and mix well.
6. Keep aside in warm place until dough rises in bulk.
7. Add the pearl sugar and gently, stir to combine.
8. Keep aside for about 13-15 minutes.
9. Set your waffle iron and lightly, grease it.
10. Add 3 tbsp of the dough of in waffle iron and cook for about 4-5 minutes.
11. Repeat with the remaining mixture.
12. Enjoy warm.

July's Zesty Waffles

Prep Time: 50 mins
Total Time: 1 hr 5 mins

Servings per Recipe: 1
Calories   308.3
Fat   11.9g
Cholesterol   131.7mg
Sodium   442.8mg
Carbohydrates   41.6g
Protein   9.5g

Ingredients

1 3/4 C. all-purpose flour, sifted
2 tsp baking powder
1/2 tsp baking soda
1/4 tsp salt
1 lemon, zest, grated
1 3/4 C. low-fat milk
1/4 C. melted butter
3 eggs, separated
2 tbsp icing sugar

Directions

1. In a bowl, add the flour, baking soda, baking powder and salt and mix well.
2. Now, sift the flour mixture into another bowl.
3. Add the lemon zest and mix well.
4. In another bowl, add the egg yolks, butter and milk and beat until well combined.
5. With a spoon, create a well in the center of the flour mixture.
6. Slowly, add the flour mixture in the well and mix until just blended.
7. With a plastic sheet, cover the bowl and
8. keep aside for about 30 minutes.
9. Set your waffle iron and lightly, grease it.
10. In a glass bowl, add the egg whites and beat until fluffy.
11. Slowly, add the icing sugar, beating continuously until soft peaks form.
12. Gently, fold the whipped egg whites into the flour mixture.
13. Add desired amount of the mixture in waffle iron and cook as suggested by the manufacturer.
14. Repeat with the remaining mixture.
15. Enjoy warm.

APPLE, WALNUTS, and Pumpkin Waffles

Prep Time: 10 mins
Total Time: 40 mins

Servings per Recipe: 6
Calories   249.5
Fat   8.9g
Cholesterol   36.9mg
Sodium   301.7mg
Carbohydrates   33.7g
Protein   8.5g

Ingredients

1 large egg, beaten
2 egg whites, beaten
4 tbsp brown sugar
1 C. evaporated skim milk
2 tbsp vegetable oil
1/2 C. pumpkin puree, canned
2 tsp vanilla
1 C. all-purpose flour
2 tsp baking powder
1/4 tsp salt

1 1/2 tsp cinnamon
1/2 tsp nutmeg
1/4 tsp ginger
1/4 tsp clove
1/2 C. apple, diced
1/4 C. toasted walnuts

Directions

1. Set your waffle iron and lightly, grease it.
2. In a bowl, add the flour, baking powder and salt and mix well.
3. In another bowl, add the pumpkin, sugar, oil, milk, egg, egg whites and vanilla and beat until well combined.
4. Add the flour mixture and mix until just combined.
5. Gently, fold in the walnuts and apple.
6. Add 3/4 C. of the mixture in waffle iron and cook as suggested by the manufacturer.
7. Repeat with the remaining mixture.
8. Enjoy warm.

Florida Duplex Waffles with Vanilla Syrup

Prep Time: 25 mins
Total Time: 45 mins

Servings per Recipe: 8
Calories 429.2
Fat 12.5g
Cholesterol 83.4mg
Sodium 325.8mg
Carbohydrates 72.0g
Protein 8.8g

Ingredients

2 C. all-purpose flour
1 tbsp sugar
2 tsp baking powder
1/2 tsp salt
3 eggs, separated
2 C. milk
1/4 C. vegetable oil
Syrup
1 C. sugar

1/2 C. light corn syrup
1/4 C. water
1 (5 oz.) cans evaporated milk
1 tsp vanilla extract
1/2 tsp ground cinnamon

Directions

1. In a bowl, add the sugar, flour, baking powder and salt.
2. Add the oil, milk and egg yolks and mix until just combined.
3. In a glass bowl, add the egg whites and beat until stiff peak form.
4. Gently, fold the whipped egg whites into the flour mixture.
5. Add desired amount of the mixture in waffle iron and cook as suggested by the manufacturer.
6. Repeat with the remaining mixture.
7. In the meantime, for the syrup: in a pot, add the corn syrup, sugar and water over medium heat and cook until boiling.
8. Cook for until desired thickness of the syrup.
9. Remove from the heat and immediately, stir in the milk, cinnamon and vanilla.
10. Enjoy the waffles alongside the syrup.

WAFFLES
Stockholm

Prep Time: 10 mins
Total Time: 25 mins

Servings per Recipe: 2
Calories   894.4
Fat   45.4g
Cholesterol   505.7mg
Sodium   308.5mg
Carbohydrates   100.8g
Protein   21.7g

Ingredients

4 eggs
100 g sugar
120 g flour
200 ml sour cream

3 tbsp butter, melted
1 tsp ground cardamom

Directions

1. In a bowl, add the sugar and eggs and beat until fluffy.
2. Add the sour cream, flour and cardamom and mix until well combined.
3. Add the butter and mix well.
4. Keep aside for about 15 minutes.
5. Set your waffle iron and lightly, grease it.
6. Add desired amount of the mixture in waffle iron and cook as suggested by the manufacturer.
7. Repeat with the remaining mixture.
8. Enjoy warm.

Gingery Pumpkin Waffles

Prep Time: 10 mins
Total Time: 15 mins

Servings per Recipe: 4
Calories 585.5
Fat 18.5g
Cholesterol 222.6mg
Sodium 1053.9mg
Carbohydrates 84.7g
Protein 19.9g

Ingredients

2 1/2 C. all-purpose flour
1/4 C. brown sugar
2 tsp baking powder
1 tsp baking soda
1/2 tsp kosher salt
2 tsp ground cinnamon
1 tsp ground ginger
1/2 tsp ground cloves
4 large eggs

2 1/2 C. shaken buttermilk
4 tbsp melted butter
1 C. pumpkin puree
Confectioners' sugar

Directions

1. Set your waffle iron and lightly, grease it.
2. In a bowl, add the flour, brown sugar, baking soda, baking powder, spices and salt and mix well.
3. Now, sift the flour mixture into a second bowl.
4. In a third bowl, add the butter, buttermilk, eggs and pumpkin and beat until well combined.
5. Add the flour mixture and mix until blended nicely.
6. Add desired amount of the mixture in waffle iron and cook as suggested by the manufacturer.
7. Repeat with the remaining mixture.
8. Enjoy warm with a dusting of the confectioners' sugar.

WILLIE MAE'S
Buttermilk Waffles

Prep Time: 10 mins
Total Time: 25 mins

Servings per Recipe: 4
Calories   176.9
Fat   4.5g
Cholesterol   2.4mg
Sodium   700.1mg
Carbohydrates   26.8g
Protein   6.8g

Ingredients

3/4 C. all-purpose flour
1/4 C. cornmeal
1 tsp baking soda
1/2 tsp salt
1 C. buttermilk
1 tbsp canola oil

2 egg whites
1 tbsp vanilla
1/2 C. wheat germ

Directions

1. Set your waffle iron and lightly, grease it.
2. In a bowl, add the flour, cornmeal, baking soda and salt and mix well.
3. In another bowl, add the oil, buttermilk and vanilla and beat until well combined.
4. Add the flour mixture and mix until well combined.
5. In a glass bowl, add the egg whites and beat until stiff peak form.
6. Gently, fold the whipped egg whites into the flour mixture.
7. Add desired amount of the mixture in waffle iron and cook as suggested by the manufacturer.
8. Repeat with the remaining mixture.
9. Enjoy warm.

Rochester Lemon Waffles

Prep Time: 30 mins
Total Time: 45 mins

Servings per Recipe: 1
Calories 309.7
Fat 19.4g
Cholesterol 195.2mg
Sodium 157.8mg
Carbohydrates 25.7g
Protein 8.2g

Ingredients

5 eggs
1/4 C. sugar
1 C. flour, sifted
1 tsp lemon juice,
1/2 tsp lemon peel, grated

1 C. sour cream
1/4 C. butter

Directions

1. In a bowl, add the sugar and eggs and beat until mixture becomes fluffy.
2. Add the flour, sour cream and lemon peel and mix until well combined.
3. Add the lemon juice and butter and mix until well combined.
4. Keep aside for about 12-15 minutes.
5. Set your waffle iron and lightly, grease it.
6. Add 3/4 C. of the mixture in waffle iron and cook for about 50-60 seconds per side.
7. Repeat with the remaining mixture.
8. Enjoy warm.

SPELMAN
Seltzer Waffles

Prep Time: 5 mins
Total Time: 15 mins

Servings per Recipe: 1
Calories	65.6
Fat	6.0g
Cholesterol	33.8mg
Sodium	164.1mg
Carbohydrates	1.2g
Protein	1.7g

Ingredients

2 1/4 C. spelt flour
1 tbsp baking powder
1/4 tsp salt
2 eggs
1 C. milk

3/4 C. seltzer water
1/4 C. oil

Directions

1. Set your waffle iron and lightly, grease it.
2. In a bowl, add the flour, baking powder and salt and mix well.
3. Add the remaining ingredients and mix until well combined.
4. Add desired amount of the mixture in waffle iron and cook for about 3-5 minutes.
5. Repeat with the remaining mixture.
6. Enjoy warm.

London Butterscotch Waffles

Prep Time: 1 hr
Total Time: 1 hr

Servings per Recipe: 6
Calories   480.6
Fat   14.0g
Cholesterol   113.8mg
Sodium   426.7mg
Carbohydrates   77.0g
Protein   11.6g

Ingredients

- 2 1/4 C. flour
- 1/2 tsp baking powder
- 1/2 tsp baking soda
- 1/2 tsp salt
- 1 tsp cinnamon
- 1/2 tsp nutmeg
- 1/4 C. brown sugar, packed
- 3 eggs, separated
- 2 C. sour milk
- 2 ripe bananas, mashed well
- 1 C. butterscotch chips

Directions

1. In a bowl, add the flour, brown sugar, baking soda, baking powder, spices and salt and mix well.
2. Now, sift the flour mixture into another bowl.
3. In a separate bowl, add the egg yolks and beat.
4. Add the bananas and sour milk and beat until well combined.
5. Add the flour mixture and mix until combined nicely.
6. In a glass bowl, add the egg whites and beat until stiff peak form.
7. Gently, fold the whipped egg whites into the flour mixture.
8. Now, gently fold in the butterscotch chips.
9. Set your waffle iron and lightly, grease it.
10. Add desired amount of the mixture in waffle iron and cook as suggested by the manufacturer.
11. Repeat with the remaining mixture.
12. Enjoy warm.

WAFFLES
Augusta Autumn

Prep Time: 5 mins
Total Time: 25 mins

Servings per Recipe: 4
Calories   413.1
Fat   10.8g
Cholesterol   163.7mg
Sodium   600.0mg
Carbohydrates   65.1g
Protein   14.1g

Ingredients

1 3/4 C. flour
2 tsp baking powder
3 tsp sugar
1/2 tsp salt
3 eggs, separated

1 1/2 C. milk
1/3 C. applesauce
1 C. whipped cream
1 C. canned peaches in light syrup

Directions

1. Set your waffle iron and lightly, grease it.
2. In a bowl add the flour, sugar, baking powder and salt and mix well.
3. In another bowl, add the milk and egg yolks and beat until blended nicely.
4. Add the flour mixture and mix until well combined.
5. Add the applesauce and mix until well combined.
6. In a glass bowl, add the egg whites and beat until stiff peak form.
7. Gently, fold the whipped egg whites into the flour mixture.
8. Add 2/3 C. of the mixture in waffle iron and cook for about 3-4 minutes.
9. Repeat with the remaining mixture.
10. Enjoy warm with a topping of the peach slices and whipped cream.

Corn on Oats Waffles

Prep Time: 10 mins
Total Time: 40 mins

Servings per Recipe: 4
Calories	531.7
Fat	19.9 g
Cholesterol	93.6 mg
Sodium	871.7 mg
Carbohydrates	73.9 g
Protein	14.8 g

Ingredients

1 large egg
2 2/3 C. buttermilk
1 1/3 C. unbleached all-purpose flour
2/3 C. regular rolled oats
2/3 C. cornmeal
1 1/4 tsp baking soda
1/4 tsp salt

3 tbsp sugar
1/3 C. melted butter, cooled

Directions

1. In a bowl, add the flour, oats, cornmeal, baking soda, sugar and salt and mix well.
2. In another bowl, crack the egg and beat.
3. Add the buttermilk and beat until well combined.
4. Add the flour mixture and mix until just combined.
5. Add the butter and stir until just combined.
6. Add 2/3 C. of the mixture in waffle iron and cook as suggested by the manufacturer.
7. Repeat with the remaining mixture.
8. Enjoy warm.

COFFEE
Bisquick Waffles

Prep Time: 15 mins
Total Time: 30 mins

Servings per Recipe: 4
Calories 459.5
Fat 24.1g
Cholesterol 53.8mg
Sodium 694.0mg
Carbohydrates 52.9g
Protein 9.2g

Ingredients

1 (1/8 oz.) packet instant coffee
1/3 C. hot water
2 C. baking mix (Bisquick)
1/3 C. miniature chocolate chip
1 C. whole milk

1 large egg
2 tbsp vegetable oil
syrup
1/4 C. miniature chocolate chip

Directions

1. Set your waffle iron and lightly, grease it.
2. In a bowl, add the coffee packet and 1/3 C. of the hot water and mix until well combined.
3. Add the chocolate morsels, baking mix, egg, oil and milk and beat until blended nicely.
4. Add desired amount of the mixture in waffle iron and cook as suggested by the manufacturer.
5. Repeat with the remaining mixture.
6. Enjoy warm with a topping of the chocolate morsels.

Poppy Seed Waffles

Prep Time: 20 mins
Total Time: 30 mins

Servings per Recipe: 4
Calories   661.8
Fat   18.2g
Cholesterol   173.0mg
Sodium   736.1mg
Carbohydrates   115.0g
Protein   13.5g

Ingredients

Berry Glaze
1 lb. frozen blueberries, thawed and undrained
6 tbsp apple juice
1/2 C. sugar
1 tbsp cornstarch
1 tbsp lemon juice
Waffles
1 1/2 C. all-purpose flour
6 tbsp sugar
2 tbsp poppy seeds
1 1/2 tsp baking powder
1 tsp baking soda
1/4 tsp salt
3 large eggs
1 1/4 C. buttermilk
1/4 C. unsalted butter, melted
1 tbsp grated lemon, rind

Directions

1. For the sauce: in a heavy-bottomed pan, add the sugar, blueberries and 1/2 C. of the apple juice over medium heat and cook until boiling. Cook for about 14-15 minutes, stirring occasionally.
2. In a bowl, add the remaining 2 tbsp of the apple juice and 1 tbsp of the cornstarch and mix until well combined.
3. Add the cornstarch mixture into the blueberry mixture and stir to combine. Stir in the lemon juice and cook until boiling, mixing continuously. Cook for about 1 minute.
4. Remove from the heat and keep aside to cool.
5. For the waffles: in a bowl, add the flour, sugar, poppy seeds, baking powder, baking soda and salt and mix well.
6. In another bowl, add the butter, buttermilk, eggs and lemon peel and beat until well combined.
7. Add the flour mixture and mix until just combined.
8. Keep aside for about 13-15 minutes.

9. Add desired amount of the mixture in waffle iron and cook for about 7 minutes.
10. Repeat with the remaining mixture.
11. Enjoy warm with a topping of the blueberry sauce.

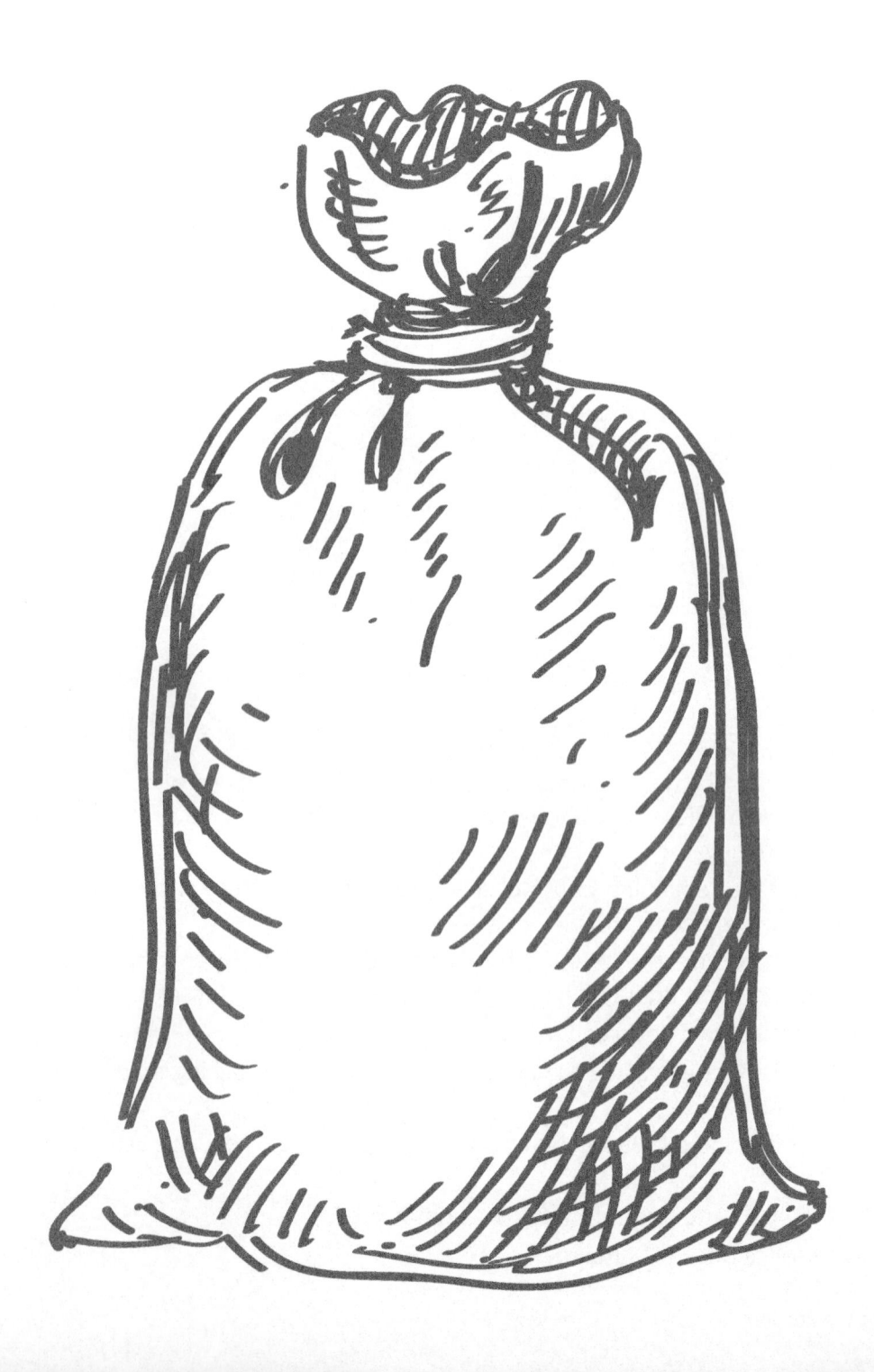

Citrus Waffles

Prep Time: 10 mins
Total Time: 20 mins

Servings per Recipe: 4
Calories   466.7
Fat   18.2g
Cholesterol   246.3mg
Sodium   731.4mg
Carbohydrates   60.9g
Protein   14.1g

Ingredients

- 2 C. flour
- 3 tsp baking powder
- 2 tbsp sugar
- 1/2 tsp salt
- 4 eggs
- 1/2 C. milk
- 1/2 C. pulp free orange juice
- 4 tbsp melted butter
- 3 tbsp grated orange zest

Directions

1. Set your waffle iron and lightly, grease it.
2. In a bowl, add the flour, sugar, baking powder and salt and mix well.
3. Now, sift the flour mixture into another bowl.
4. In another bowl, add the eggs, butter, milk and orange juice and beat until well combined.
5. Add the orange zest and stir to combine.
6. Add the flour mixture and mix until well combined.
7. Add desired amount of the mixture in waffle iron and cook as suggested by the manufacturer.
8. Repeat with the remaining mixture.
9. Enjoy warm.

CHOCO CHIP
Waffles

🥣 Prep Time: 5 mins
🕐 Total Time: 15 mins

Servings per Recipe: 8
Calories 321.2
Fat 15.4g
Cholesterol 49.0mg
Sodium 323.6mg
Carbohydrates 40.3g
Protein 7.1g

Ingredients

2 C. all-purpose flour
2 tbsp sugar
1 tbsp baking powder
1/2 tsp salt
1 2/3-2 C. low-fat milk

1 medium banana, mashed
6 tbsp vegetable oil
2 large eggs
1/2 C. mini chocolate chip

Directions

1. In a bowl, add the flour, sugar, baking powder and salt and mix well.
2. Add the remaining ingredients and mix until combined nicely.
3. Keep aside for about 4-5 minutes before cooking.
4. Set your waffle iron and lightly, grease it.
5. Add 1/2 C. of the mixture in waffle iron and cook for about 2 minutes.
6. Repeat with the remaining mixture.
7. Enjoy warm.

Alternative Pancakes

Prep Time: 12 mins
Total Time: 12 mins

Servings per Recipe: 4
Calories   230 kcal
Fat   8.2 g
Carbohydrates   32.7 g
Protein   6.4 g
Cholesterol   65 mg
Sodium   650 mg

Ingredients

- 3/4 C. milk
- 2 tbsp white vinegar
- 1 C. all-purpose flour
- 2 tbsp white sugar
- 1 tsp baking powder
- 1/2 tsp baking soda
- 1/2 tsp salt
- 1 egg
- 2 tbsp butter, melted
- cooking spray

Directions

1. In a medium bowl, mix together the milk and vinegar and keep aside for about 5 minutes.
2. In a large bowl, mix together the flour, sugar, baking powder, baking soda and salt.
3. Add the egg and butter into the milk mixture and beat to combine.
4. Add the flour mixture into the milk mixture and beat till no lumps are here.
5. Grease a large skillet with cooking spray and heat on medium heat.
6. Add about 1/4 C of the mixture into the skillet and cook till the bubbles form on the surface.
7. With a spatula, flip and cook till browned from this side.
8. Repeat with the remaining mixture.

PANCAKES
for Autumn

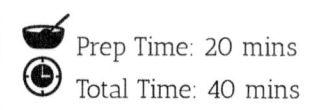

Prep Time: 20 mins
Total Time: 40 mins

Servings per Recipe: 6
Calories	278 kcal
Fat	7.2 g
Carbohydrates	45.8g
Protein	7.9 g
Cholesterol	36 mg
Sodium	608 mg

Ingredients

- 1 1/2 C. milk
- 1 C. pumpkin puree
- 1 egg
- 2 tbsp vegetable oil
- 2 tbsp vinegar
- 2 C. all-purpose flour
- 3 tbsp brown sugar
- 2 tsp baking powder
- 1 tsp baking soda
- 1 tsp ground allspice
- 1 tsp ground cinnamon
- 1/2 tsp ground ginger
- 1/2 tsp salt

Directions

1. In a bowl, add the milk, pumpkin, egg, oil and vinegar and beat till well combined.
2. In another large bowl, mix together the flour, brown sugar, baking powder, baking soda, allspice, cinnamon, ginger and salt.
3. Add the flour mixture into pumpkin mixture and mix till just combine.
4. Heat a lightly greased griddle on medium-high heat.
5. Add about 1/4 C of the mixture into the griddle and cook till browned from both sides.
6. Repeat with the remaining mixture.
7. Serve hot.

Dutch Pancakes

Prep Time: 10 mins
Total Time: 30 mins

Servings per Recipe: 2
Calories	392 kcal
Fat	23.8 g
Carbohydrates	33.4g
Protein	11.7 g
Cholesterol	237 mg
Sodium	509 mg

Ingredients

- 3 tbsp butter
- 1/2 C. all-purpose flour
- 1/2 C. milk
- 2 eggs, beaten
- 1 tsp white sugar
- 1/4 tsp salt
- 1/4 lemon, juiced (optional)
- 1 tbsp confectioners' sugar

Directions

1. Set your oven to 425 degrees F before doing anything else.
2. In a 9-inch pie plate, add the butter and place the plate in the preheating oven for about 5-10 minutes.
3. In a bowl, add the flour, milk, eggs, white sugar and salt and beat till well combined.
4. Transfer the mixture into the pie plate over hot butter evenly.
5. Cook in the oven for about 20-24 minutes or till a toothpick inserted in the center comes out clean.
6. Drizzle the pancake with lemon juice and serve with a sprinkling of the confectioners' sugar.

LIGHT
Pancakes

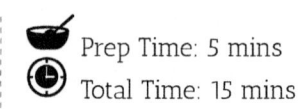

Prep Time: 5 mins
Total Time: 15 mins

Servings per Recipe: 3
Calories	264 kcal
Fat	5.1 g
Carbohydrates	48.9 g
Protein	5.4 g
Cholesterol	0 mg
Sodium	717 mg

Ingredients

1 1/4 C. all-purpose flour
2 tbsp white sugar
2 tsp baking powder
1/2 tsp salt

1 1/4 C. water
1 tbsp oil

Directions

1. In a large bowl, mix together the flour, sugar, baking powder and salt.
2. In a small bowl, add the water and oil and beat to combine.
3. Make a well in the center of the flour mixture.
4. Add the oil mixture into the well and mix till just combined.
5. Heat a lightly greased griddle on medium-high heat.
6. With a large spoonfuls, place the mixture into the griddle and cook till the bubbles form on the surface.
7. Flip and cook till browned from the other side.
8. Repeat with the remaining mixture.

Sourdough Pancakes

Prep Time: 10 mins
Total Time: 30 mins

Servings per Recipe: 12
Calories	117 kcal
Fat	7.2 g
Carbohydrates	10.7g
Protein	2.5 g
Cholesterol	32 mg
Sodium	232 mg

Ingredients

- 1 C. all-purpose flour
- 3/4 tsp baking soda
- 1/2 tsp salt
- 2 tbsp white sugar
- 1 tsp baking powder
- 1 C. Herman Sourdough Starter
- 1/3 C. vegetable oil
- 2 eggs
- 1/2 C. milk

Directions

1. In a large bowl, mix together the flour, baking soda, salt, sugar and baking powder.
2. Add the sourdough starter, oil, eggs and milk and beat till well combined.
3. Heat a lightly greased griddle on medium-high heat.
4. Add about 1/4 C of the mixture into the griddle and cook till browned from both sides.
5. Repeat with the remaining mixture.
6. Serve hot.

POTATO
Pancakes

Prep Time: 15 mins
Total Time: 45 mins

Servings per Recipe: 15
Calories	197 kcal
Fat	2.4 g
Carbohydrates	39 g
Protein	5.2 g
Cholesterol	37 mg
Sodium	652 mg

Ingredients

5 lb. potatoes, peeled
1 onion
3 eggs, beaten
2 1/2 C. dry pancake mix
2 tsp salt
1 tsp ground black pepper

1 tbsp vegetable oil

Directions

1. In a food processor, add the potatoes and onion and pulse till grated.
2. In a large bowl, mix together the potatoes, onions, eggs, pancake mix, salt and pepper.
3. In a large skillet, heat the oil on medium heat.
4. Add the desired amount of potato mixture and cook for about 3-4 minutes per side.
5. Repeat with the remaining mixture.

Authentic Austrian Pancakes

Prep Time: 15 mins
Total Time: 50 mins

Servings per Recipe: 6
Calories   316 kcal
Fat   21.7 g
Carbohydrates   23.3g
Protein   7.5 g
Cholesterol   151 mg
Sodium   205 mg

Ingredients

- 1 C. all-purpose flour
- 1/4 tsp salt
- 2 tbsp sugar
- 1 C. milk
- 3 eggs
- 1 C. heavy cream
- 2 tbsp margarine

Directions

1. Set your oven to 325 degrees F before doing anything else.
2. In a bowl, mix together the flour, salt and sugar.
3. Add the milk, eggs and cream and mix till a smooth mixture forms.
4. In a cast iron skillet, melt the margarine.
5. Transfer the mixture into the skillet over the melted margarine evenly.
6. Cook in the oven for about 35 minutes or till a toothpick inserted in the center comes out clean.
7. Remove from the oven, and keep aside to cool till the pancake sets.
8. Serve with a drizzling of the maple syrup.

TRADITIONAL
Swedish Pancakes

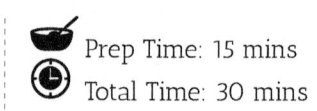

Prep Time: 15 mins
Total Time: 30 mins

Servings per Recipe: 4
Calories	382 kcal
Fat	19.8 g
Carbohydrates	34.1g
Protein	16.5 g
Cholesterol	225 mg
Sodium	459 mg

Ingredients

4 extra large eggs, separated
1 C. all-purpose flour
1/2 tsp salt
2 tbsp white sugar
1 C. milk
3 tbsp sour cream

4 egg whites
3 tbsp vegetable oil

Directions

1. In a bowl, add the egg yolks and beat till thick.
2. In another bowl, sift together the flour, salt and sugar.
3. Add the flour mixture and milk into the egg yolks alternately and mix till just combined.
4. Stir in the sour cream.
5. In a third bowl, add the egg whites and beat till stiff but not dry.
6. Fold the egg whites into the mixture.
7. In a skillet, heat a small amount of the oil on high heat.
8. Add about 1 tbsp of the mixture into the skillet and tilt the pan to spread the mixture evenly.
9. Cook till the pancake browns from one side.
10. Flip the pancake and cook till browned from the other side.
11. Repeat with the remaining mixture.

March
Brunch Pancakes

Prep Time: 15 mins
Total Time: 50 mins

Servings per Recipe: 8
Calories	360 kcal
Fat	19.5 g
Carbohydrates	31.2g
Protein	15.1 g
Cholesterol	89 mg
Sodium	792 mg

Ingredients

- 2 C. baking mix (such as Bisquick (R))
- 2 C. shredded Cheddar cheese, divided
- 1 C. milk
- 5 tbsp maple syrup
- 2 eggs
- 1 1/2 tbsp white sugar
- 12 slices cooked turkey bacon, crumbled

Directions

1. Set your oven to 350 degrees F before doing anything else and grease a 13x9-inch baking dish.
2. In a bowl, add the baking mix, 1 C. of the Cheddar cheese, milk, maple syrup, eggs and sugar and mix till well combined.
3. Transfer the mixture into the prepared baking dish.
4. Cook in the oven for about 20-25 minutes or till a toothpick inserted in the center comes out clean.
5. Remove from the oven and top the casserole with the bacon and remaining 1 C. of the Cheddar cheese evenly.
6. Cook in the oven for about 5 minutes.

3-INGREDIENT Fruit Banana Pancakes

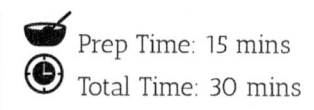

Prep Time: 15 mins
Total Time: 30 mins

Servings per Recipe: 4
Calories 93 kcal
Fat 2.7 g
Carbohydrates 14.9 g
Protein 3.8 g
Cholesterol 93 mg
Sodium 36 mg

Ingredients

1 banana, mashed
1 egg
1 tsp arrowroot powder

Directions

1. In a blender, add the banana, egg and arrowroot powder and pulse till well combined.
2. Heat a griddle on medium heat.
3. Place half of the mixture into the griddle and cook for about 2-3 minutes per side.
4. Repeat with the remaining mixture.

Turkish Pancakes

Prep Time: 15 mins
Total Time: 1 hr 20 mins

Servings per Recipe: 8
Calories   86 kcal
Fat   3.5 g
Carbohydrates   10g
Protein   3.5 g
Cholesterol   48 mg
Sodium   124 mg

Ingredients

2/3 C. water
2/3 C. milk
2 eggs
1 tbsp vegetable oil

1/3 tsp salt
3/4 C. all-purpose flour

Directions

1. In a bowl, add the water, milk, eggs, vegetable oil and salt and beat till well combined.
2. Slowly, add the flour into egg mixture and beat till well combined.
3. Keep the mixture aside for about 1 hour.
4. Stir the mixture again.
5. Heat a lightly greased griddle on medium-high heat.
6. Add the mixture by large spoonfuls into the griddle and cook for about 2-4 minutes per side.
7. Repeat with the remaining mixture.

HEALTHY BREAKFAST
Pancakes

Prep Time: 10 mins
Total Time: 20 mins

Servings per Recipe: 4
Calories   304 kcal
Fat   2.7 g
Carbohydrates   64.6 g
Protein   9.6 g
Cholesterol   0 mg
Sodium   734 mg

Ingredients

2 C. white whole wheat flour
2 tbsp baking powder
2 tbsp ground flax meal
17 fluid oz. orange juice

1 tsp orange extract

Directions

1. In a bowl, mix together the flour, baking powder and flax meal.
2. Add the orange juice and orange extract into flour mixture and mix till well-combined.
3. Heat a lightly greased griddle on medium-high heat.
4. Add the mixture by large spoonfuls into the griddle and cook for about 3-4 minutes.
5. Flip and cook for about 2-3 minutes.
6. Repeat with the remaining mixture.

Apple Cinnamon Pancakes

Prep Time: 15 mins
Total Time: 30 mins

Servings per Recipe: 2
Calories	654 kcal
Fat	28.4 g
Carbohydrates	86 g
Protein	16.6 g
Cholesterol	421 mg
Sodium	525 mg

Ingredients

- 3 tbsp butter
- 1 large apple, cored and sliced
- 1/2 C. white sugar, divided
- 2 tsp ground cinnamon
- 4 eggs
- 1/3 C. milk
- 1/3 C. all-purpose flour
- 1 tsp baking powder
- 1 tsp vanilla extract
- 1 pinch salt

Directions

1. Set your oven to 400 degrees F before doing anything else.
2. In an oven proof skillet, melt the butter on medium heat.
3. Add the apple slices, 1/4 C. of the sugar and cinnamon and cook, stirring for about 5 minutes.
4. Meanwhile in a large bowl, add the eggs, milk, flour, remaining 1/4 C. of the sugar, baking powder, vanilla extract and salt and beat till smooth.
5. Place the mixture over the apple slices evenly.
6. Cook in the oven for about 10 minutes.
7. Remove from the oven and run a spatula around the edges of the pancake to loosen.
8. Invert the skillet over a large plate and serve.

PEANUT BUTTER Chocolate Pancakes

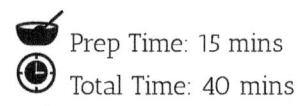

Prep Time: 15 mins
Total Time: 40 mins

Servings per Recipe: 4
Calories	484 kcal
Fat	23.4 g
Carbohydrates	58.2g
Protein	13.5 g
Cholesterol	77 mg
Sodium	737 mg

Ingredients

1 1/4 C. all-purpose flour
1 tbsp baking powder
1/2 tsp salt
2 tbsp brown sugar
1 1/2 C. milk
1 egg, beaten

3 tbsp butter, melted
1 tsp vanilla extract
1/4 C. peanut butter
1/4 C. chocolate chips
1 ripe banana, diced

Directions

1. In a bowl, mix together the flour, baking powder, salt and brown sugar.
2. In another bowl, add the egg and milk and beat till well combined.
3. Add the peanut butter and stir till smooth.
4. Add the milk mixture into the flour mixture and mix till just moistened.
5. Add the melted butter and vanilla extract and beat to combine.
6. Gently fold in the chocolate chips and diced banana.
7. Heat a large nonstick skillet on medium heat.
8. Add about 1/4 C. of the mixture into the skillet and cook for about 2 minutes.
9. Flip and cook for about 2-3 minutes.
10. Repeat with the remaining mixture.

Chicken Pancakes

Prep Time: 6 mins
Total Time: 21 mins

Servings per Recipe: 4
Calories	321 kcal
Fat	17.8 g
Carbohydrates	9.6g
Protein	29.1 g
Cholesterol	116 mg
Sodium	441 mg

Ingredients

- 1 lb. skinless, boneless chicken breast meat - finely chopped
- 1/2 medium onion, finely chopped
- 3 tbsp mayonnaise
- 1 egg, lightly beaten
- 1/3 C. all-purpose flour
- salt and pepper to taste
- 2 tbsp vegetable oil

Directions

1. In a large bowl, add the chicken, onion, mayonnaise, egg, flour, salt and pepper and mix till well combined.
2. In a skillet, heat the oil on medium heat.
3. Add about 1/4 C. of the chicken mixture into the skillet and cook till browned from both sides.
4. Repeat with the remaining mixture.
5. Serve hot.

TRUE TUSCAN
Pancakes

Prep Time: 5 mins
Total Time: 20 mins

Servings per Recipe: 4
Calories   350 kcal
Fat   24.9 g
Carbohydrates   15g
Protein   16.7 g
Cholesterol   61 mg
Sodium   681 mg

Ingredients

3/4 C. baking mix (such as Bisquick (R))
1/3 C. water
1 (8 oz.) package Cheddar cheese, shredded

5 tsp prepared pesto

Directions

1. Heat a greased griddle.
2. In a bowl, add the baking mix, water, Cheddar cheese and pesto and mix till well combined.
3. Add about 1/4 C. of the mixture into the griddle and cook for about 2-3 minutes per side.
4. Repeat with the remaining mixture.

Buckwheat Buttermilk Pancakes

Prep Time: 10 mins
Total Time: 25 mins

Servings per Recipe: 4
Calories	196 kcal
Fat	5.8 g
Carbohydrates	25.7g
Protein	9.1 g
Cholesterol	57 mg
Sodium	444 mg

Ingredients

- 1 C. buckwheat flour
- 1 1/2 tsp white sugar
- 1 tsp baking powder
- 1/4 tsp salt
- 1/4 tsp baking soda
- 1 1/4 C. buttermilk
- 1 large egg, beaten
- 1/4 tsp vanilla extract
- 1 tbsp unsalted butter

Directions

1. In a bowl, mix together the buckwheat flour, sugar, baking powder, salt and baking soda.
2. In another bowl, add the buttermilk, egg and vanilla extract and beat till well combined.
3. Add the flour mixture into the buttermilk mixture and beat till the mixture becomes thick and smooth.
4. Keep the mixture aside for about 5 minutes.
5. In a griddle, melt the butter on medium heat.
6. Add the mixture by large spoonfuls into the griddle and cook for about 3-4 minutes.
7. Flip and cook for about 2-3 minutes.

ALMOND Amaranth Pancakes

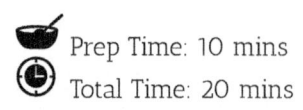

Prep Time: 10 mins
Total Time: 20 mins

Servings per Recipe: 4
Calories   273 kcal
Fat   3.9 g
Carbohydrates 50.9 g
Protein   8.6 g
Cholesterol   46 mg
Sodium   185 mg

Ingredients

1/2 C. rice flour
1/2 C. sorghum flour
1/2 C. amaranth
1 tsp baking powder
1 tsp ground cinnamon
1 C. almond milk

1/2 C. unsweetened applesauce
1 egg
cooking spray

Directions

1. In a bowl, mix together the rice flour, sorghum flour, amaranth, baking powder and cinnamon.
2. Add the almond milk, applesauce and egg into flour mixture and mix till just combined.
3. Grease a griddle with cooking spray and heat on medium heat.
4. Add the mixture by large spoonfuls into the griddle and cook for about 3-4 minutes.
5. Flip and cook for about 2-3 minutes.
6. Repeat with the remaining mixture.

Pancakes in Scotland

Prep Time: 15 mins
Total Time: 25 mins

Servings per Recipe: 12
Calories	219 kcal
Fat	7.4 g
Carbohydrates	30.7 g
Protein	7.2 g
Cholesterol	63 mg
Sodium	515 mg

Ingredients

- 3 C. all-purpose flour
- 3 tbsp white sugar
- 3 tsp baking powder
- 1 1/2 tsp baking soda
- 3/4 tsp salt
- 3 C. buttermilk
- 1/2 C. milk
- 3 eggs
- 1/3 C. butter, melted

Directions

1. In a large bowl, mix together the flour, sugar, baking powder, baking soda and salt.
2. In another bowl, add the buttermilk, milk, eggs and melted butter and beat till well combined.
3. Keep the both mixtures separate just before cooking.
4. Heat a lightly greased griddle on medium-high heat.
5. Add the eggs mixture into the flour mixture and mix till just combined.
6. Add about 1/2 C. of the mixture into the griddle and cook till browned from both sides.
7. Repeat with the remaining mixture.
8. Serve hot.

BUTTERMILK
Oat Pancakes

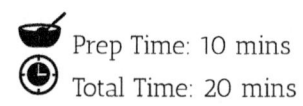

Prep Time: 10 mins
Total Time: 20 mins

Servings per Recipe: 4
Calories	207 kcal
Fat	9.3 g
Carbohydrates	24.6g
Protein	6 g
Cholesterol	48 mg
Sodium	605 mg

Ingredients

1/2 C. all-purpose flour
1/2 C. quick cooking oats
1 tbsp white sugar
1 tsp baking powder
1/2 tsp baking soda
1/2 tsp salt

3/4 C. buttermilk
1 tsp vanilla extract
2 tbsp vegetable oil
1 egg

Directions

1. In a food processor, add the flour, oats, sugar, baking powder, baking soda, salt, buttermilk, vanilla, oil and egg and pulse till smooth.
2. Heat a lightly greased griddle on medium-high heat.
3. Add about 1/4 C. of the mixture into the griddle and cook till browned from both sides.
4. Repeat with the remaining mixture.
5. Serve hot.

Wednesday's Breakfast Pancakes

Prep Time: 20 mins
Total Time: 50 mins

Servings per Recipe: 4
Calories   548 kcal
Fat   29.5 g
Carbohydrates   57.2 g
Protein   17 g
Cholesterol   163 mg
Sodium   1079 mg

Ingredients

- 1 C. whole wheat flour
- 2/3 C. all-purpose flour
- 1/3 C. wheat germ
- 1 1/2 tsp baking powder
- 1/2 tsp baking soda
- 2 tbsp brown sugar
- 1 tsp salt
- 5 1/3 tbsp cold unsalted butter
- 2 1/2 C. buttermilk
- 2 eggs, beaten
- 3 tbsp unsalted butter

Directions

1. In a food processor, add the whole wheat flour, white flour, wheat germ, baking powder, baking soda, brown sugar and salt.
2. With a knife, cut the cold butter into small pieces into the flour-mixture and mix till a sand-like mixture forms.
3. Make a well in the center of the flour mixture.
4. Add the buttermilk and eggs into the well and stir till well combined.
5. Grease a frying pan with 1 tbsp of the butter and heat on medium heat.
6. Add the desired amount of the mixture into the pan to form a 4-inch pancakes and cook till the bubbles form on the surface.
7. Flip and cook for about 2 minutes.
8. Repeat with the remaining mixture.

DECEMBER'S
German Pancakes

🥣 Prep Time: 25 mins
🕐 Total Time: 45 mins

Servings per Recipe: 6
Calories	283 kcal
Fat	11 g
Carbohydrates	40.7g
Protein	6.8 g
Cholesterol	62 mg
Sodium	246 mg

Ingredients

2 eggs
2 tbsp all-purpose flour
1/4 tsp baking powder
1/2 tsp salt
1/4 tsp pepper
6 medium potatoes, peeled and shredded
1/2 C. finely chopped onion
1/4 C. vegetable oil

Directions

1. In a large bowl, add the eggs, flour, baking powder, salt and pepper and beat till well combined.
2. Stir in the potatoes and onion.
3. In a large skillet, heat oil on medium heat.
4. Add the mixture by heaping tbsps into the skillet and press to flatten.
5. Cook for about 3 minutes per side.
6. Transfer onto paper towel lined plate to drain.
7. Repeat with the remaining mixture.

How to Make a Pancakes

🍲 Prep Time: 5 mins
🕐 Total Time: 25 mins

Servings per Recipe: 4
Calories   318 kcal
Fat   11.9 g
Carbohydrates   43.7g
Protein   9 g
Cholesterol   75 mg
Sodium   1119 mg

Ingredients

1 1/2 C. all-purpose flour
3 1/2 tsp baking powder
1 tsp salt
1 tbsp white sugar
3 tbsp butter, melted
1 egg
1 1/4 C. milk

cooking spray

Directions

1. In a large bowl, sift together the flour, baking powder, salt and sugar.
2. Add the melted butter, egg and milk and beat till just combined.
3. Keep aside the mixture for about 5 minutes.
4. Grease a large skillet with the cooking spray and heat on medium-high heat.
5. Add about 1/4 C. of the mixture and cook for about 2-3 minutes.
6. Flip and cook for about 1-2 minutes.
7. Repeat with the remaining mixture.

POTATO BUTTERMILK
Pancakes

Prep Time: 20 mins
Total Time: 35 mins

Servings per Recipe: 10
Calories   147 kcal
Fat   5.8 g
Carbohydrates   20.4g
Protein   3.1 g
Cholesterol   29 mg
Sodium   269 mg

Ingredients

1 C. rice flour
3 tbsp tapioca flour
1/3 C. potato starch
4 tbsp dry buttermilk powder
1 packet sugar substitute
1 1/2 tsp baking powder
1/2 tsp baking soda
1/2 tsp salt
1/2 tsp xanthan gum
2 eggs
3 tbsp canola oil
2 C. water

Directions

1. In a bowl, sift together the rice flour, tapioca flour, potato starch, dry buttermilk powder, sugar substitute, baking powder, baking soda, salt and xanthan gum.
2. Add the eggs, water and oil and stir till well combined but a few lumps remain.
3. Heat a large greased skillet on medium-high heat.
4. Add the desired amount of the mixture into the skillet and cook till the bubbles begin to form.
5. Flip and cook till golden brown on bottom.
6. Serve immediately with a topping of your favorite condiments.

Friday's Flax Blueberry Pancakes

Prep Time: 5 mins
Total Time: 5 mins

Servings per Recipe: 4
Calories	332 kcal
Fat	9.5 g
Carbohydrates	50.8g
Protein	12.4 g
Cholesterol	94 mg
Sodium	791 mg

Ingredients

- 1 1/2 C. dry pancake mix
- 1/2 C. flax seed meal
- 1 C. skim milk
- 2 eggs
- 1 C. fresh blueberries

Directions

1. Heat a nonstick skillet on medium heat.
2. In a bowl, mix together the pancake mix and flax seed meal.
3. In another bowl, add the milk and eggs and beat till well combined.
4. Add the milk mixture into the pancake mix mixture and stir till just moistened.
5. Add about 1/4 C. of the mixture into the skillet and sprinkle with 1/4 C. of the blueberries.
6. Cook till the bubbles form on the surface.
7. Flip and cook till browned from the other side.
8. Repeat with the remaining mixture.

GOURMET
Pancake Crepes

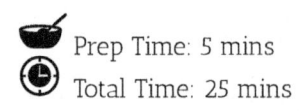

🥣 Prep Time: 5 mins
🕐 Total Time: 25 mins

Servings per Recipe: 2
Calories   241 kcal
Fat   21.8 g
Carbohydrates   2.4g
Protein   < 9.6 g
Cholesterol   238 mg
Sodium   215 mg

Ingredients

3 oz. cream cheese, softened
2 eggs, beaten
1 tsp ground cinnamon
1 tbsp sugar-free syrup

1 tsp butter

Directions

1. In a bowl, add the cream cheese.
2. Add the beaten eggs, about 1 tsp at a time at first and mash till a smooth mixture forms.
3. Add the cinnamon and sugar-free syrup and beat to combine.
4. In a nonstick skillet, melt the butter on medium heat.
5. After the butter has stopped foaming, reduce the heat to medium-low.
6. Add the mixture by several tbsp and swirl to coat the bottom of the skillet.
7. Cook for about 4 minutes.
8. Flip the crepe with a spatula and cook for about 1-2 minutes.
9. Repeat with the remaining mixture.

Zucchini Cheddar Pancakes

Prep Time: 20 mins
Total Time: 35 mins

Servings per Recipe: 6
Calories	207 kcal
Fat	12.5 g
Carbohydrates	15.4g
Protein	8.9 g
Cholesterol	82 mg
Sodium	397 mg

Ingredients

- 2 C. grated zucchini
- 1 C. shredded Cheddar cheese
- 1/2 C. grated onion
- 2 eggs, beaten
- 1 C. biscuit baking mix (such as Bisquick(R))
- 2 tsp vegetable oil

Directions

1. In a bowl, mix together the zucchini, Cheddar cheese and onion.
2. Add the eggs and biscuit mix and mix till well combined.
3. In a griddle, heat the vegetable oil on medium heat.
4. Add about 1/4 C. of the mixture into the griddle and cook for about 3-4 minutes per side.
5. Repeat with the remaining mixture.

RUSSIAN Breakfast Pancakes

Prep Time: 15 mins
Total Time: 1 hr 5 mins

Servings per Recipe: 8
Calories	525 kcal
Fat	26.4 g
Carbohydrates	57.1 g
Protein	14.4 g
Cholesterol	153 mg
Sodium	378 mg

Ingredients

4 1/4 C. milk
5 eggs
1/3 tsp salt
2 tbsp white sugar
1/2 tsp baking soda
1/8 tsp citric acid powder
4 C. all-purpose flour
3 tbsp vegetable oil
1 C. boiling water
2/3 C. butter, divided

Directions

1. In a bowl, add the milk and eggs and beat well.
2. Add the salt and the sugar and mix till well combined.
3. Add the flour, baking soda and citric acid and mix to combine.
4. Slowly, add the vegetable oil and boiling water, stirring continuously till a very thin mixture forms.
5. Keep the mixture aside for about 20 minutes.
6. In a small frying pan, melt 1 tbsp of the butter on medium-high heat.
7. Remove the pan from the heat and immediately, add the mixture by a ladleful and tilt the pan to spread the mixture in a thin circle.
8. Return the pan to the heat and cook for about 90 seconds.
9. Carefully, flip and cook for about 1 minute.
10. Transfer the blini into a kitchen towel lined plate.
11. Repeat with the remaining butter and the mixture.
12. Stack them on top of each other and cover with the kitchen towel to keep warm.
13. Place your favorite filling in the center of the blini and fold three times to make a triangle shape.
14. You can also fold up all 4 sides, like a small burrito.

Louisiana Inspired Pancakes

Prep Time: 15 mins
Total Time: 35 mins

Servings per Recipe: 4
Calories   309 kcal
Fat   14 g
Carbohydrates   38g
Protein   8.5 g
Cholesterol   72 mg
Sodium   865 mg

Ingredients

- 2 tsp canola oil, divided
- 2 C. diced apples
- 2 tbsp white sugar, divided
- 2 tsp ground cinnamon
- 3/4 C. milk
- 2 tbsp melted butter
- 1 egg
- 1 1/2 tsp bourbon whiskey, optional
- 1/2 tsp vanilla extract
- 1/2 C. all-purpose flour
- 1/2 C. oat flour
- 1 tbsp baking powder
- 1/2 tsp salt
- 2 tbsp chopped cooked turkey bacon

Directions

1. In a skillet, heat 1 tsp of the canola oil on medium heat and cook the apples, 1 tbsp of the gar and cinnamon for about 5-10 minutes.
2. Remove the skillet from the heat.
3. Win a bowl, add the milk, butter, egg, bourbon and vanilla extract and beat till well combined.
4. In another bowl, sift together the all-purpose flour, oat flour, 1 tbsp of the sugar, baking powder and salt.
5. Add the flour mixture into the milk mixture and mix till well combined.
6. Fold in the apples and bacon.
7. In a skillet, heat remaining 1 tsp of the canola oil on medium heat.
8. Add about 1/2 C. of the mixture into the skillet and cook for about 3-5 minutes per side.
9. Repeat with the remaining mixture.

OCTOBER'S
Pancakes

🥣 Prep Time: 20 mins
🕐 Total Time: 20 mins

Servings per Recipe: 10
Calories	271 kcal
Fat	5.2 g
Carbohydrates	52.9 g
Protein	3.6 g
Cholesterol	40 mg
Sodium	260 mg

Ingredients

Pancakes:
1 C. Original Bisquick(R) mix
1 C. Betty Crocker(R) SuperMoist(R) yellow cake mix
3 tbsp candy sprinkles
1 C. milk
1 tsp vanilla
2 eggs

Glaze and Garnish:
2 1/2 C. powdered sugar
3 tbsp milk plus
2 tsp milk
1 tsp vanilla
Additional candy sprinkles

Directions

1. Heat a greased griddle on medium-high heat.
2. In a bowl, add the pancake
3. Ingredients and mix till well combined.
4. Add 1/4 C. of the mixture into the griddle and cook till the edges become dry.
5. Flip and cook till golden brown.
6. Repeat with the remaining mixture.
7. Stack on serving plates.
8. In small bowl, add the powdered sugar, milk and 1/2 tsp of the vanilla and beat till smooth.
9. Serve with a topping of the glaze and additional candy sprinkles.

Rustic Country Squash Pancakes

Prep Time: 15 mins
Total Time: 30 mins

Servings per Recipe: 8
Calories	107 kcal
Fat	5.7 g
Carbohydrates	10.6 g
Protein	3.9 g
Cholesterol	49 mg
Sodium	255 mg

Ingredients

- 2 tbsp chicken stock
- 2 eggs, slightly beaten
- 1 C. baking mix (such as Bisquick(R))
- 4 pattypan squash, grated
- 1/4 C. diced onion
- 1/4 C. grated Parmesan cheese
- 1 tsp minced garlic
- 1/2 C. vegetable oil

Directions

1. In a bowl, add the chicken stock and eggs and beat to combine.
2. Add the baking mix and beat till just moistened.
3. Add the squash, onion, Parmesan cheese and garlic and stir till well combined.
4. Keep aside for about 5 minutes.
5. In a large skillet, heat the oil to 350 degrees F.
6. Add about 1/4 C. of the mixture into the hot oil and cook for about 2-3 minutes per side.
7. Repeat with the remaining mixture.
8. Transfer pancakes to a brown paper bag-lined surface to drain.

ALABAMA PORCH
Pancakes

🥣 Prep Time: 15 mins
🕐 Total Time: 25 mins

Servings per Recipe: 12
Calories   214 kcal
Fat   8.2 g
Carbohydrates   31g
Protein   6.1 g
Cholesterol   18 mg
Sodium   396 mg

Ingredients

1 1/2 C. old-fashioned rolled oats
1 1/2 C. whole wheat flour
2 tsp baking soda
1 tsp baking powder
1/2 tsp salt
1/2 tsp ground cinnamon
1/4 tsp ground nutmeg
1 1/2 C. buttermilk
1 C. milk
1/3 C. white sugar
1/4 C. vegetable oil
1 egg
1/2 C. raisins
3 tbsp chopped walnuts
1 tsp vegetable oil

Directions

1. In a food processor, add the oats and pulse till finely ground.
2. In a bowl, mix together the grounded oats, flour, baking soda, baking powder, salt, cinnamon and nutmeg.
3. In another bowl, add the buttermilk, milk, sugar, 1/4 C. of the vegetable oil and egg and beat till smooth.
4. Add the egg mixture into the oat mixture and mix till well combined.
5. Fold in the raisins and walnuts.
6. Grease a griddle with remaining 1 tsp of the oil and heat on medium heat.
7. Add the mixture by large spoonfuls into the griddle and cook for about 3-4 minutes.
8. Flip and cook for about 2-4 minutes.
9. Repeat with the remaining mixture.

Loveable Fruity Pancakes

Prep Time: 10 mins
Total Time: 20 mins

Servings per Recipe: 8
Calories   202 kcal
Fat   9.6 g
Carbohydrates   25.8g
Protein   4.7 g
Cholesterol   26 mg
Sodium   211 mg

Ingredients

Crisco(R) Original No-Stick Cooking Spray
1 large egg, slightly beaten
2/3 C. milk
2 tbsp Crisco(R) Pure Canola Oil
1 (7 oz.) package Martha White(R) Banana Nut Flavored Muffin Mix
1 C. low-fat vanilla yogurt
2 C. berries, sliced strawberries, blueberries and raspberries
Powdered sugar (optional)

Directions

1. Grease a griddle with the cooking spray and heat it.
2. In a bowl, add the egg, milk, oil and muffin mix in medium bowl and mix till large lumps disappear.
3. Add about 1/4 C. of the mixture into the hot griddle and cook for about 1-2 minutes per side.
4. Repeat with the remaining mixture.
5. Place the yogurt and berries over half of each pancake and fold over.
6. Serve with a sprinkling of the powdered sugar

GARDEN ZUCCHINI
Pancakes

Prep Time: 15 mins
Total Time: 20 mins

Servings per Recipe: 8
Calories   392 kcal
Fat   23.3 g
Carbohydrates   37.1g
Protein   8.2 g
Cholesterol   77 mg
Sodium   607 mg

Ingredients

2 tbsp olive oil
2 C. shredded zucchini
2 C. finely crushed buttery round crackers (such as Ritz(R))
1 1/2 C. finely chopped yellow onion
3 eggs, beaten
1/2 C. shredded sharp Cheddar cheese
salt and ground black pepper to taste

Directions

1. In a large skillet, heat the oil on medium-high heat.
2. In a bowl, add the zucchini, crackers, onion, eggs, Cheddar cheese, salt and pepper and mix till well combined.
3. Shae the zucchini mixture into small equal sized patties.
4. Cook the patties in the hot oil for about 2-3 minutes per side.

Swedish Breakfast

Prep Time: 10 mins
Total Time: 40 mins

Servings per Recipe: 4
Calories   301 kcal
Fat   10.2 g
Carbohydrates   36.2g
Protein   15.3 g
Cholesterol   159 mg
Sodium   892 mg

Ingredients

- 4 slices turkey bacon, cut into 1x1/2-inch squares
- 3 eggs
- 2 tbsp white sugar
- 1 tsp salt
- 2 C. milk
- 1 C. all-purpose flour

Directions

1. Set the broiler of your oven and arrange oven rack about 6-inches from the heating element.
2. In a 13x9-inch baking dish, spread the bacon squares and cook under the broiler for about 7-10 minutes.
3. Now, set your oven to 425 degrees F.
4. In a bowl, add the eggs, sugar and salt and beat well.
5. Add the milk and flour alternately, mixing till a thin mixture forms.
6. Transfer the mixture into the hot baking dish with the bacon.
7. Cook in the oven for about 20-30 minutes.

I ♥ Pancakes

Prep Time: 10 mins
Total Time: 20 mins

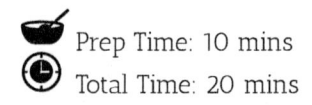

Servings per Recipe: 2
Calories   386 kcal
Fat   10.6 g
Carbohydrates   63.5g
Protein   7.8 g
Cholesterol   93 mg
Sodium   35 mg

Ingredients

1 C. rice flour
salt to taste
1 egg, beaten
1 tbsp vegetable oil
1 tbsp water

cooking spray

Directions

1. In a bowl, mix together the rice flour and salt.
2. Make a well in the center of the flour mixture.
3. Add the egg, vegetable oil and enough water in the well and mix till a smooth mixture forms.
4. Grease a non-stick frying pan with cooking spray and heat on medium heat.
5. Add about 1/4 C. of the mixture and tilt pan to cover the bottom with a thin pancake.
6. Cook for about 1 minute per side.
7. Repeat with the remaining mixture.

Tropical Coconut Pancakes

Prep Time: 5 mins
Total Time: 10 mins

Servings per Recipe: 1
Calories	682 kcal
Fat	48.7 g
Carbohydrates	51.3g
Protein	20.7 g
Cholesterol	372 mg
Sodium	140 mg

Ingredients

2 eggs
1/4 C. coconut flour
2 tbsp coconut oil, melted
1 1/8 tbsp stevia sweetener
1/2 tsp vanilla extract
1 tsp coconut oil

Directions

1. In a bowl, add the eggs, coconut flour, 2 tbsp of the melted oil, stevia sweetener and vanilla extract and beat till smooth.
2. In a large skillet, melt 1 tsp of the coconut oil on medium heat.
3. Add enough mixture into the skillet and cook for about 2-3 minutes per side.

TRADITIONAL Chinese Pancakes

Prep Time: 30 mins
Total Time: 1 hr 10 mins

Servings per Recipe: 8
Calories   120 kcal
Fat   5.5 g
Carbohydrates   15.4g
Protein   2.1 g
Cholesterol   0 mg
Sodium   75 mg

Ingredients

1/4 tsp salt
3/4 C. warm water
1 C. all-purpose flour
1/4 tsp vegetable oil (optional)
1/4 C. all-purpose flour
1 tbsp vegetable oil
1 tbsp Asian (toasted) sesame oil
1/2 C. finely chopped green onion
1 tbsp vegetable oil

Directions

1. In a bowl, dissolve the salt in warm water.
2. Add 1 C. of the flour and mix till a soft dough forms.
3. Place the dough out onto a well-floured smooth surface and knead for about 5 minutes.
4. Divide the dough into 8 equal-size portions and keep aside covered with a cloth.
5. In a bowl, add 1/4 C. of the flour and 1 tbsp of the vegetable oil and mix till a fine crumbs like mixture forms.
6. Place 1 portion of dough onto a floured smooth surface and roll into a 5x7-inch thin square.
7. Coat the dough with toasted sesame oil and lightly, sprinkle with about 1 1/2 tsp of the flour-oil mixture.
8. Sprinkle about 1 tbsp of chopped green onion onto the dough and spread the onion out evenly.
9. Starting with a long end, roll the dough up into a rope shape, and pinch the seam and the ends closed.
10. Roll the rope shape into a flat spiral and with your hands, press lightly to compact the spiral and keep it from unrolling.
11. Place the spiral down onto the floured work surface and gently roll it out into a 5-inch diameter pancake with the onions folded inside, turning the pancake over often. (Avoid making holes in the pancakes.)
12. Repeat with the remaining dough portions.
13. Grease a non-stick skillet with vegetable oil and heat on medium heat.
14. Cook each pancake for about 5 minutes per side.
15. Cut into the wedges and serve warm.

Parsnip Pancakes

Prep Time: 10 mins
Total Time: 25 mins

Servings per Recipe: 2
Calories	194 kcal
Fat	13 g
Carbohydrates	14.7g
Protein	5.8 g
Cholesterol	138 mg
Sodium	641 mg

Ingredients

- 1 C. grated peeled parsnips
- 2 small eggs
- 1/4 C. finely chopped onion
- 1 tbsp olive oil
- 1/2 tsp salt
- 1/2 tsp dried rosemary
- ground black pepper to taste (optional)
- 1 tsp sunflower oil

Directions

1. In a bowl, add the parsnips, eggs, onion, olive oil, salt, rosemary and black pepper and mix till a lumpy mixture forms.
2. In a heavy frying pan, heat the sunflower oil on medium heat.
3. Add the desired amount of the mixture into oil and cook for about 6-7 minutes per side.

SOUTH INDIAN
Pancakes

Prep Time: 15 mins
Total Time: 1 hr 5 mins

Servings per Recipe: 8
Calories   119 kcal
Fat   2.8 g
Carbohydrates   21.2g
Protein   2.9 g
Cholesterol   0 mg
Sodium   4 mg

Ingredients

1 C. brown rice flour
1/2 C. whole wheat flour
1 1/2 C. water
1 red onion, finely chopped
1 clove garlic, minced
1/4 C. fresh cilantro, chopped
1/4 tsp white sugar
1/2 tsp ground turmeric
1 tsp ground cumin
2 tsp whole mustard seeds
1 tsp cumin seeds
1 tsp ground coriander
1 tsp ground ginger
1 pinch cayenne pepper
3 tbsp rice vinegar
1 tbsp vegetable oil

Directions

1. In a bowl, mix together the brown rice and whole wheat flour.
2. Add the water and mix till a thin mixture forms.
3. Add the onion, garlic, cilantro, sugar, turmeric, cumin, mustard seeds, cumin seeds, coriander, ginger, cayenne pepper and rice vinegar and mix till well combined.
4. Refrigerate, covered for at least 1/2 hour or overnight.
5. In a skillet, heat the oil on medium heat.
6. Add about 1/4 C. of the mixture into the oil and tilt the skillet to spread the mixture in a thin layer in the bottom.
7. Cook for about 1 minute per side.
8. Repeat with the remaining mixture.

Spinach Pancakes

Prep Time: 10 mins
Total Time: 20 mins

Servings per Recipe: 4
Calories	145 kcal
Fat	9.8 g
Carbohydrates	9.3g
Protein	6.6 g
Cholesterol	93 mg
Sodium	88 mg

Ingredients

- 4 tbsp all-purpose flour
- 2 eggs
- 1 (10 oz.) package frozen spinach, thawed and drained
- salt and pepper to taste
- 1/2 tsp paprika
- 2 tbsp olive oil

Directions

1. In a bowl, add the flour and eggs and mix till well combined.
2. Stir in the spinach, salt, pepper and paprika.
3. In a large skillet, heat the olive oil.
4. Place the spinach mixture by the spoonful into the skillet and flatten into patties.
5. Cook till browned from both sides.
6. Transfer onto paper towel lined plate to drain.
7. Repeat with the remaining mixture.
8. Serve warm.

CARROT Pancakes

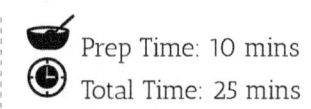

Prep Time: 10 mins
Total Time: 25 mins

Servings per Recipe: 60
Calories	16 kcal
Fat	< 1 g
Carbohydrates	1.3g
Protein	< 0.5 g
Cholesterol	< 9 mg
Sodium	39 mg

Ingredients

oil for frying
2 C. grated carrots
6 green onions, chopped
1/2 C. all-purpose flour
1/2 tsp baking powder
3 eggs
3/4 tsp salt
1 pinch freshly ground black pepper

Directions

1. In a large pan, add about 1/2-inch deep oil and heat to 350 degrees F.
2. In a bowl, add the carrots, green onion, flour and baking powder and mix till the carrots are coated completely.
3. In another bowl, add the eggs, salt and pepper and beat well.
4. Add the egg mixture into the carrot mixture and stir till moistened.
5. In batches, place small mounds of carrot mixture into the hot oil and cook for about 2-3 minutes per side.
6. With a slotted spoon, transfer the latkes onto a paper towel-lined plate to drain.

Veggie Combo Pancakes

Prep Time: 15 mins
Total Time: 30 mins

Servings per Recipe: 6
Calories   94 kcal
Fat   7.9 g
Carbohydrates   5.8g
Protein   1.6 g
Cholesterol   20 mg
Sodium   65 mg

Ingredients

3 zucchini
1 large onion
1 tsp dried oregano
salt and pepper to taste
1/4 C. butter

Directions

1. Grate the zucchini and onion and transfer into a bowl.
2. Drain off the excess moisture from the bowl.
3. Add the oregano, salt and pepper and stir to combine.
4. In a frying pan, melt the butter on medium-high heat.
5. Add desired amount of the zucchini mixture in a flat layer in the pan and cook for about 5 minutes per side.
6. Serve warm.

SPICY BUFFALO Chicken Pancakes

Prep Time: 15 mins
Total Time: 30 mins

Servings per Recipe: 12
Calories   207 kcal
Fat   8.9 g
Carbohydrates   25g
Protein   6.6 g
Cholesterol   59 mg
Sodium   713 mg

Ingredients

2 frozen, breaded chicken strips
3 tbsp hot sauce (such as Frank's RedHot (R))
6 C. leftover mashed potatoes
3 eggs
1 (1 oz.) package ranch dressing mix
2 tbsp vegetable oil

1/2 C. shredded Cheddar cheese

Directions

1. Cook the chicken strips according to package's instructions.
2. Chop the cooked chicken strips and transfer into a bowl.
3. Add the hot pepper sauce and toss to coat well.
4. In a large bowl, add the mashed potatoes, eggs and ranch dressing mix and stir till well combined.
5. In a large skillet, heat the oil on medium heat.
6. Add about 1/2 C. of the potato mixture into the skillet and press to flatten.
7. Sprinkle a heaping tbsp of the cooked chicken strips over the pancake and cook for about 4 minutes per side.
8. Serve with a garnishing of the shredded cheese.

Country Cottage Pancakes

Prep Time: 10 mins
Total Time: 15 mins

Servings per Recipe: 7
Calories	142 kcal
Fat	9.5 g
Carbohydrates	3.3g
Protein	10.6 g
Cholesterol	136 mg
Sodium	244 mg

Ingredients

1 1/2 C. cottage cheese
1 C. eggs
2 tbsp all-purpose flour
2 tbsp coconut oil
1/2 tsp vanilla extract

Directions

1. In a blender, add the cottage cheese, eggs, flour, coconut oil and vanilla extract and pulse till smooth.
2. Heat a lightly greased griddle on medium-high heat.
3. Add the mixture by large spoonfuls into the griddle and cook for about 3-4 minutes.
4. Flip and cook for about 2-3 minutes.
5. Repeat with the remaining mixture.

SOUTH AFRICAN
Pancakes

Prep Time: 15 mins
Total Time: 1 hr

Servings per Recipe: 4
Calories   292 kcal
Fat   6.2 g
Carbohydrates   52.6 g
Protein   7.9 g
Cholesterol   46 mg
Sodium   60 mg

Ingredients

1 beet, cooked
1 C. all-purpose flour, sifted
1 C. milk
1 egg
1 tbsp vegetable oil
1 tsp white vinegar (optional)
2 tsp ground cinnamon

1/4 C. white sugar
2 oranges, quartered

Directions

1. In a food processor, add the cooked beet, flour, milk, egg, vegetable oil and vinegar and pulse till smooth.
2. Transfer the mixture into a bowl and keep aside for about 30 minutes.
3. In a small bowl, mix together the cinnamon and sugar.
4. Heat a greased non-stick skillet on medium heat.
5. Add the enough mixture and tilt the skillet till the mixture covers the bottom evenly.
6. Cook till the mixture turns moist and the edges begin to curl away from the sides of the skillet.
7. Flip and cook till lightly golden from the other side.
8. Place the pancake onto a plate and cover with a kitchen towel to keep moist.
9. Repeat with the remaining mixture.
10. Sprinkle the cinnamon sugar over the pancakes and roll them.
11. Serve with the orange quarters.

Cocoa Chocolate Pancakes

Prep Time: 5 mins
Total Time: 13 mins

Servings per Recipe: 4
Calories	418 kcal
Fat	17.2 g
Carbohydrates	59.2g
Protein	11.7 g
Cholesterol	114 mg
Sodium	257 mg

Ingredients

- 1 1/4 C. all-purpose flour
- 1/4 C. unsweetened cocoa powder
- 3 tbsp white sugar
- 1/4 tsp salt
- 2 eggs, at room temperature
- 1 1/4 C. milk
- 1/2 tsp vanilla
- 2 tbsp melted butter
- 1/2 C. semisweet chocolate chips

Directions

1. Large bowl, mix together the flour, cocoa powder, sugar and salt.
2. In another bowl, add the eggs, milk and vanilla and beat till well combined.
3. Stir in the melted butter.
4. Add the egg mixture into the flour mixture and mix till just combined.
5. Fold in the chocolate chips.
6. Heat a lightly greased griddle on medium-high heat.
7. Add about 1/4 C. of the mixture into the griddle and cook for about 2-3 minutes.
8. Flip and cook for about 1 minute.
9. Repeat with the remaining mixture.

NORTHERN CALIFORNIA
Pancakes

Prep Time: 15 mins
Total Time: 45 mins

Servings per Recipe: 8
Calories   231 kcal
Fat   9.2 g
Carbohydrates   31.9 g
Protein   4.7 g
Cholesterol   49 mg
Sodium   567 mg

Ingredients

1 egg
3 tbsp butter, melted
1 tbsp vanilla extract
1 tbsp white sugar
1 1/4 C. milk
1/4 C. heavy cream
1 1/2 C. all-purpose flour
3 1/2 tsp baking powder
1 tsp salt
1/4 C. white sugar
2 tbsp brown sugar
1/4 tsp ground cinnamon
1 tsp butter

Directions

1. In a bowl, add the egg, 3 tbsp of the melted butter, vanilla extract and 1 tbsp of the white sugar and beat till well combined.
2. Add the milk and cream and beat to combine.
3. In another bowl, sift together the flour, baking powder and salt.
4. Add the flour mixture into the egg mixture and mix till a smooth mixture forms.
5. In a small bowl, mix together 1/4 C. of the white sugar, brown sugar and cinnamon.
6. In a skillet, melt 1 tsp of the butter on medium-low heat.
7. Add about 3 tbsp of the mixture into the skillet and sprinkle with about 2 tsp of the cinnamon sugar evenly.
8. Cook for about 2-3 minutes.
9. Flip and cook for about 3 minutes.
10. Repeat with the remaining mixture and cinnamon sugar.
11. Let the pancakes cool without stacking to avoid softening the sugar crust.

Sweet Pea Pancakes

Prep Time: 10 mins
Total Time: 20 mins

Servings per Recipe: 4
Calories	145 kcal
Fat	9.8 g
Carbohydrates	9.3g
Protein	6.6 g
Cholesterol	93 mg
Sodium	88 mg

Ingredients

4 tbsp all-purpose flour
2 eggs
1 (10 oz.) package frozen sweet peas, boiled and drained
salt and pepper to taste
1/2 tsp paprika
2 tbsp olive oil

Directions

1. In a bowl, add the flour and eggs and mix till well combined.
2. Stir in the peas, salt, pepper and paprika.
3. In a large skillet, heat the olive oil.
4. Place the pea mixture by the spoonful into the skillet and flatten into patties.
5. Cook till browned from both sides.
6. Transfer onto paper towel lined plate to drain.
7. Repeat with the remaining mixture.
8. Serve warm.

SIMPLE SUMMER
Pesto

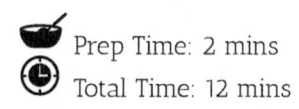

Prep Time: 2 mins
Total Time: 12 mins

Servings per Recipe: 6
Calories   199 kcal
Fat   21.1 g
Carbohydrates   2 g
Protein   1.7 g
Cholesterol   0 mg
Sodium   389 mg

Ingredients

1/4 C. almonds
3 cloves garlic
1 1/2 C. fresh basil leaves
1/2 C. olive oil
1 pinch ground nutmeg
salt and pepper to taste

Directions

1. Set your oven to 450 degrees F before doing anything else.
2. Arrange the almonds onto a cookie sheet and bake for about 10 minutes or till toasted slightly.
3. In a food processor, add the toasted almonds and the remaining ingredients till a rough paste forms.

ENJOY THE RECIPES?

KEEP ON COOKING WITH 6 MORE FREE COOKBOOKS!

Visit our website and simply enter your email address to join the club and receive your 6 cookbooks.

http://booksumo.com/magnet

https://www.instagram.com/booksumopress/

https://www.facebook.com/booksumo/

Printed in Great Britain
by Amazon